Things You Need To Know about the Holy Ghost

Part 1

The REALITY... of The PERSON... of The HOLY SPIRIT!

Volume 5

By Ernest Angley

The REALITY of The PERSON of The HOLY SPIRIT *Volume* ***5***

Things You Need to Know About the Holy Ghost, Part 1

Printed in the United States of America.
Distributed by Winston Press.
P.O. Box 2091, Akron, Ohio 44309
ISBN 978-1-935974-50-5

CONTENTS

CHAPTER 1

Who Is the Holy Ghost?

As you read this book, you must keep in mind that the Holy Spirit, the third person in the Trinity of the Godhead, is definitely a real person. Only then will you be able to get everything out of this profound revelation of Him that God wants you to have. Jesus said, **Take my yoke upon you, and learn of me** (Matthew 11:29). Now, the Lord is saying, "Learn the Holy Spirit"; and that is *thus saith the Lord*. How do you do that?—through prayer, fasting and living in the Word. Those three things will take you into the will of the Holy Spirit where you will want nothing but the will of God.

The secret of this Jesus ministry is in knowing the Holy Spirit, knowing how He works and knowing how to work with Him. Some of you have had difficulty learning to work with the Holy Spirit because you did not consider Him to be a real person.

If you are going to work with someone and do a good job, you have to know that person; and if you are going to live with someone, you have to know and have understanding of that person's personality—what makes it up and what is in it. You have to know whether or not you blend with that personality. It is beyond any plan that man could have ever come up with to have the person of the Holy Spirit in our lives, that our bodies would become His temples and that He would move into the life of each person who will prepare for Him and want Him.

The Holy Spirit is for everybody. **For the promise is unto you, and to your children, and to all that are afar off, even as many as the Lord our God shall call** (Acts 2:39). But the Holy Spirit is not an intruder. He will not invade your life and move in to live with you unless you welcome Him and prepare for Him.

What manner of person is the Holy Spirit, and what is He like? Some of you have the Holy Spirit baptism, but you are not really acquainted with Him. That is why you have no more answers than you do and why some of you are always looking to somebody else to give you answers. I do not look to people to give me answers; I look to the Holy Spirit, and I depend on Him. The Spirit will make the scriptures so real to you that you should not doubt any of them. I have no trouble believing the whole Word.

When I am going through great conflict, I hide away with the Holy Spirit. No matter how long it takes, I have to have answers; and to get answers from Heaven, you must yield to the person of the Holy Spirit. He has come to direct you in all things, but He cannot direct you unless you want to be directed; and you have to know He is there before you will let Him direct you. Some people say they want to be directed by the high arm of God, but they do not act like it. When you have the Holy Spirit, He will live with you, dine with you, help you and direct you.

A HOLY GHOST FAMILY

In my home, I learned from my family's actions and teachings. When troubles came, we did not go to the pastor for help; we took them home. There, we got answers because my parents were connected with God and because the Holy Ghost was such a reality in our home.

When the Holy Ghost hit the Angley family, it was like a bomb. He was something to reckon with, and He transformed our home. When my parents and two older sisters received the Holy Ghost, they were transformed in such glory and in such love of the Lord that I wondered, "What manner of person is this who has entered our home?"

My sister Pete was the one who first brought the Holy Ghost light into our home. She went to a little Pentecostal church one Sunday night and came home Monday morning around two o'clock and woke Mama and Daddy up crying, "I got the Holy Ghost!" Lord, they did not know whether or not there was such a thing as the Holy Ghost, but she brought Him in and blew up the place.

Mama watched Pete that week and decided she would go down to that church and see what was happening. My mama and daddy believed that you had to live free from sin; they did not believe in using tobacco in any form, and they had Jesus in their hearts. That made them candidates for the Holy Ghost.

That night, Mama hit the altar and praised God for a little while; and the Holy Ghost fell on her. Then He fell on my other sister, too; and I was there watching it all. What a sight in this world it was! I had never seen my sister and mom so happy in all their lives.

That was my introduction to the Holy Ghost in my own family, and Pete was such an example to me. When I was a child, she taught me the ways of the Lord by the way she lived, the way she prayed and the way she spent her time. Neither of my two older sisters ever went to any events of the world or played the world's music.

Because of seeing all of this, I was interested

in the Holy Ghost as a child; and I liked to see people receive Him. To me, He became the greatest experience from God that a person could ever have. I had no doubt that it had to be God speaking through the person because I could see the manifestation of Him taking over a human tongue, and I knew it could not have been the spirit of man. Surely, God gave me that thought and the understanding of it. I was eighteen years old before I received the Holy Ghost, but I knew so much about Him because I had studied people as they were seeking and receiving Him.

When it came my turn to get the Holy Ghost, it seemed He was a million miles away, not because the Holy Ghost was not real to me but because nobody had ever used my tongue. I did not know how I was ever going to give over my tongue to Him, but I knew He had to have it.

When the Holy Ghost did come in, I was so excited. It was beyond me that I had Him, that He was talking through me and that I was listening to Him speak. He was doing the talking, and I had just furnished my tongue.

THE FRUITS OF THE SPIRIT

The Bible describes the Holy Ghost with the nine fruits of the Spirit. **But the fruit of the Spirit is love, joy, peace, longsuffering, gentleness, goodness, faith, Meekness, temperance** (Galatians 5:22,23). These are the fruits that the Holy Spirit produces in one's life, and they reveal the person He is and the personality He has. He is so patient, and He has such a gentle way about Him that many times you will not even realize He is moving for you. His touch is so gentle that you will not realize He is guiding you. The goodness of Heaven is flowing continually; and as long as He can flow that goodness into your mind, you will have it working for you.

These are the Holy Spirit's fruits. He is the only one who can produce them, and He produces them right in your soul; but first, you must have the right soil. That is why the Spirit works with you to get it just right because His fruits can only be produced in perfection. The Spirit knows just how to grow the fruit so it will not be damaged and so no insects will get to it; but when you will not allow the Holy

Spirit to have what He needs to produce these fruits, then He cannot produce them. You have to desire that fruit and want the Holy Spirit to produce it in you; and you have to know that there is a holy, sacred place in your soul that is roped off, so to speak, by the Holy Spirit, a place that He uses to produce all nine fruits of the Spirit. That place is carefully cultivated so the truth can be produced.

The Holy Spirit is a real gardener, and there has never been one quite like Him; but many people are deceived into thinking that all the fruits of the Spirit are being produced in their lives when they are not. The Holy Spirit will definitely teach you about the fruits, about how they work and about their profit to Heaven. He will give you the truth about them and let you know how essential they are.

DEPEND ON THE SPIRIT

To be a member of the bridal company in this last hour, you must have the Holy Ghost and learn to depend entirely on Him. You have to be forceful against the enemy, but some of you are not. You are always leaning on the wrong thing or the wrong person, so the

Holy Spirit cannot use you or flow through you what you need to defeat the devil. It is not good to lean on people; lean on the person of the Holy Spirit because He came for that purpose. Think about all of His characteristics and how much you can trust Him; then you will know that He will never betray you.

If you want to open up and tell your whole heart to someone, tell it to the Holy Spirit. People have gotten into deep trouble by telling someone their whole heart, and then that person turned against them. Or maybe that person told a friend, and that friend shared it with his friend; and on it goes.

If you want to keep something to yourself and still talk to someone, talk to the Holy Spirit. He will make intercession to Heaven for you and pray for you. He loves you so much that He will cry for you and groan through you with great compassion. **Likewise the Spirit also helpeth our infirmities: for we know not what we should pray for as we ought: but the Spirit itself maketh intercession for us with groanings which cannot be uttered** (Romans 8:26). He is the compassionate, loveable Holy Spirit.

The more you depend on the Holy Spirit, the stronger you will become because He has come to strengthen you. Some of you think you have to talk to people about your troubles every day, but that will not work. You are not getting deliverance, strength or help because your help cometh from On High. **God is our refuge and strength, a very present help in trouble** (Psalm 46:1). **I will lift up mine eyes unto the hills, from whence cometh my help. My help cometh from the LORD** (Psalm 121:1,2). When you are full of the Holy Ghost, you do not look at the Lord only once in a while; you keep Him ever before you. You look to His love, His peace, His grace and His strength; and above all, you look to His divine blood.

The Holy Spirit has come to be your great Helper; yet some of you pass Him by daily, and that grieves Him. He came to work for you and to make life better for you. He came to flow all of Heaven to you so that you could flow it out to a lost world. He is so humble, and He will produce Heaven's humility right in your innermost being. That humility will enable you to stay humble and to do the Lord's will all the time without grumbling and complaining. The Spirit helps you to pray and fast. He is your own personal protector and teacher and your source of all truth, and He has patience to teach you if you will listen.

LET THE SPIRIT HAVE CONTROL

The lack of divine self-control, or temperance, is why some of you have so many problems. You may have human self-control, but it can fail at any time. It can be set off just as easily as striking a match, and it can go up in flames like gasoline; but that is not the way you should be. You must use divine humility and divine self-control. You may say, "I cannot stop myself from getting angry and throwing things, but I regret it afterwards." Well, that comes from self and the flesh, and the Holy Ghost is not a benefit to you. You will not recognize Him for who He is or what He is—the might, the strength and the greatness of Him—so you render Him helpless to work for you again and again. Then you blame God for some of the circumstances that develop in your life when those things are your fault because you did not give over to the Holy Spirit.

You know how to yield or give your mind over to a book you are reading or to a person you are talking to, and you know how to communicate with people; so since the Holy Spirit is a person, why can't you communicate with Him? It is because you do not recognize Him to be a person; *but now it is a must, saith the Lord.*

The hour has come that you must know the Holy Spirit so He can help you night and day. You can even turn things over to Him while you sleep; and many times, He will work it out...and it is wonderful how He will work things out in your life.

Have you ever gone to sleep and then woke up to find that everything seemed to be all right, that it was a brand-new world? The Holy Ghost had seasoned that world for you and had used the greatness of Heaven for you while you slept. You may have thought that it was the rest for your body that had done it, but it was more than that—the Holy Spirit had given you the spiritual rest that Jesus spoke of. **Come unto me, all ye that labour and are heavy laden, and I will give you rest** (Matthew 11:28).

The Lord is not seeking to push you away from Him today; He is seeking for the Holy Spirit to draw you closer to Him than you have ever thought possible. Some of you have been abused and mixed up in so much of the darkness of Lucifer. Maybe you were not personally involved, but people in your home or other relatives were; and it became a way of life for you. Now, you don't know how to get deliverance from all of that; but through the Holy Spirit's teaching, it will all become so plain.

The Lord knows everything, but He does not have His book of knowledge so He can hold things against you; He has it to help you, and He will take me into people's lives to help them. If you are sincere, the Lord wants to help you; but if you are not sincere, He cannot help you unless you turn away from that spirit. You have to be sober and not in a drunken condition or involved in that which is wrong because only then can the Lord get into your mind. It may not be exactly clear what He is doing in the beginning, but the Holy Spirit will work so patiently to clear your mind.

THE DIVINE COMFORTER

The Holy Ghost is our comforter. **But the Comforter, which is the Holy Ghost, whom the Father will send in my name, he shall teach you all things, and bring all things to your remembrance, whatsoever I have said unto you** (John 14:26). It is wonderful to have the Holy Ghost to comfort you; but some of you are so busy looking for a human being to give you comfort, love and sympathy that you pass by the Great One. He will be the one to dry your tears, but many people want a human hand to dry their tears instead. As long as that is what they want, that is what they will get; and many times, they will be disappointed. I prefer the Lord to dry my tears because He will dry them and encourage my heart. He never tells me anything to tear me down or discourage me; His talk is all of inspiration. People can fail you or give you only so much comfort, but there is no limit to the comfort the Holy Spirit can give because He has both the Son and God the Father backing Him up.

You can have the Comforter, and He comforts us in so many ways that people do not realize. Think about all of the blessings He gives us and how He clothes us, supplies our needs and puts food on the table. He gives us such wonderful gifts and talents; but I see so many people who do not yield to that comfort, and they are miserable when they could have peace. The storm can be raging all around you, but it is not on the inside of you where the Comforter is unless you allow it to be in there. Once inside, it can get into your mind; and that is bad because the Spirit cannot shut it out of your mind unless you want His help.

A TYPE OF THE HOLY SPIRIT

In Genesis 24, we read the account of Abraham sending his servant Eliezer to find a wife for his son, Isaac. In that story, Abraham is a type of God, Isaac is a type of Jesus, Eliezer is a type of the Holy Ghost, and Rebekah is a type of the Bride of Christ. Abraham didn't want Isaac to marry a Canaanite girl, so he sent Eliezer back to the country of his kindred.

And the servant took ten camels of the camels of his master, and departed; for all the goods of his master were in his hand: and he arose, and went to Mesopotamia, unto the city of Nahor. And he made his camels to kneel down without the city by a well of water at the time of the evening, even the time that women go out to draw water. And he said, O LORD God of my master Abraham, I pray thee, send me good speed this day, and shew kindness unto my master Abraham. Behold, I stand here by the well of water; and the daughters of the men of the city come out to draw water: And let it come to pass, that the damsel to whom I shall say, Let down thy pitcher, I pray thee, that I may drink; and she shall say, Drink, and I will give thy camels drink also: let the same be she that thou hast appointed for thy servant Isaac; and thereby shall I know that thou hast shewed kindness unto my master (Genesis 24:10–14). When Rebekah came to the well, she did exactly as Eliezer had prayed she would; so he knew the Lord was answering his prayer.

Then Eliezer comforted Rebekah with special, beautiful gifts that Isaac had sent with him. **And the servant brought forth jewels of silver, and jewels of gold, and raiment, and gave them to Rebekah: he gave also to her brother and to her mother precious things. And they did eat and drink, he and the men that were with him, and tarried all night; and they rose up in the morning, and he said, Send me away unto my master. And they said, We will call the damsel, and inquire at her mouth. And they called Rebekah, and said unto her, Wilt thou go with this man? And she said, I will go. And Rebekah arose, and her damsels, and they rode upon the camels, and followed the man: and the servant took Rebekah, and went his way** (Genesis 24:53,54,57,58,61).

Eliezer had given Rebekah expensive gifts which gave her great comfort in knowing that she would have a good life ahead of her. That comfort also gave her full assurance that she should go with Eliezer the servant, the Holy Ghost.

Today, the Holy Spirit is a servant who has

been sent by God to serve us and to find a bride for His Son, Jesus. The Spirit gives us comfort by giving us such wonderful blessings and gifts that we know we will be all right. We drink from the wells of salvation that will never run dry. **Therefore with joy shall ye draw water out of the wells of salvation** (Isaiah 12:3).

THE COMFORTER WILL SEE YOU THROUGH

I don't know how people get along in life without the Holy Ghost. What would I have done if I had not had the Comforter when the Lord took my wife, Angel, home to be with Him? I was in millions of pieces, and I thought I would never laugh again and have it be for real. I thought I couldn't go on breathing without her. She had been so much life, strength and encouragement to me; then suddenly she was gone. The Lord had tried to tell me that He was going to take her, but I refused to believe it. I just had one little lamb, and I thought that surely He wouldn't take her...but He did.

I had always been fluent of speech, but my words started to skip. For the first time, I couldn't talk to God; and I had never thought a time would come when I couldn't even pray.

The Bible says, **In the world ye shall have tribulation: but be of good cheer; I have overcome the world** (John 16:33). I was in great tribulation, and I was in the deepest valley I had ever been in. Momentarily, I lost the vision the Holy Ghost gave of taking the Gospel to the world. I was as one dead; and for the first time, I wanted to die. I thought it was awful for anybody to want to die, but all was dark for me. Then the Lord spoke and said, "It was my divine will to have taken Angel when I did. By me taking her, she will bring more souls into my Kingdom than if I had left her with you." If I had ever believed God, I had to believe Him then.

Through it all, the Comforter would put me to sleep; and that was a relief because I didn't care if I ever woke up again. However, I knew I had to live for my congregation and for the people who were yet to come. Then one day, the Comforter came. I don't know whether it was an angel, Jesus or the Holy Spirit; but He put His arm around me just like a human arm and held me close. He comforted me and gave me vision of the fact that I had to continue on. I was on a divine mission, and I had to finish it; so I rose up determined more than ever to pay the price to win the lost at any cost.

I learned so much about the Holy Spirit in those days. I learned to let Him dry my tears with the love handkerchief of Heaven. I learned to listen and watch and realize that He was my guide every day. He was mine, living on the inside; and He would never leave me.

Once you have the Holy Ghost, He will never leave you if you live holy. That is the greatest plan that has ever been given—salvation and the Holy Ghost. He anoints us with a spirit of gladness. **Therefore God, even thy God, hath anointed thee with the oil of gladness above thy fellows** (Hebrews 1:9).

You should never think of God as being afar off. When the Lord gets ready to take people home who are ready to go, they just have to take one step; and they are there. There is no death valley to walk through. Only part of the twenty-third Psalm is for us today because

Jesus took the shadow out of death when He conquered death, hell and the grave for the Bride. **So when this corruptible shall have put on incorruption, and this mortal shall have put on immortality, then shall be brought to pass the saying that is written, Death is swallowed up in victory. O death, where is thy sting? O grave, where is thy victory** (I Corinthians 15:54,55)? When Jesus comes, He will bring our loved ones with Him; and that will be glorious!

THE SPIRIT BRINGS LIVING WATER

Jesus said, **He that believeth on me, as the scripture hath said, out of his belly shall flow rivers of living water** (John 7:38). *He that believeth on me* means that you have to believe Jesus Christ is the Son of God, your Redeemer and your Savior. You must believe He is all He claimed to be, and He claimed to be so much.

Jesus used the word "believeth," and every word in the English language that ends with *eth* means to continue on and on; so you must continue to believe. Jesus also said, *Out of his belly shall flow rivers of living water.*

Salvation is not enough; you must have the Holy Ghost for those rivers to flow. We are so blessed to have these rivers of living water flowing so mightily on the inside of us that they have to go forth. The Lord does not send them for us to contain them all.

But this spake he of the Spirit [the Holy Ghost], **which they that believe on him should receive: for the Holy Ghost was not yet given; because that Jesus was not yet glorified** (John 7:39). People can receive if they will believe on Him.

Jesus had full assurance, but some of you do not have full assurance that the Lord really cares for you and that He is with you and helping you. He sent the Holy Ghost to comfort you; but you are too busy thinking about what awful shape you are in, that you can never amount to anything and that you are not going to make it.

When you think negative thoughts, the Holy Spirit moves over and gives you plenty of room to think them. You push Him aside, and those thoughts take up the space in your life that He is supposed to have. You put Him in the back room, so to speak; and many times you lock the door. You will not yield to Him because you are too busy wallowing in your feelings when the Bible tells us we are to live by faith, not by our feelings. **For therein is the righteousness of God revealed from faith to faith: as it is written, The just shall live by faith** (Romans 1:17).

The Holy Spirit lives in us through faith, not through feelings. If He has come in, He is there whether you feel like He is or not unless you have willfully sinned against Him.

JESUS HAD TO LEAVE

Jesus gave the disciples a wonderful introduction to the Holy Spirit. **But when the Comforter is come, whom I will send unto you from the Father, even the Spirit of truth, which proceedeth from the Father, he** [the Spirit] **shall testify of me** (John 15:26). That promise is also for today.

Nevertheless I tell you the truth; It is expedient [necessary] **for you that I go away: for if I go not away, the Comforter will not come unto you; but if I depart, I will send him unto you** (John 16:7). When man sinned and degraded himself, he had to have a Savior; but he would also have to have the Spirit of truth living inside of him in the form of the person of the Holy Spirit. It was so essential for the disciples to have Him that it was necessary for Jesus, the Great One who had come down from Heaven, to leave; yet many don't feel any need of the Holy Ghost. Jesus had been born of the Virgin Mary and had walked and talked with the disciples. He had protected them, delivered them and set their feet on the right paths. Then He told them it was necessary for Him to leave or the Holy Ghost would not come, and the Spirit is essential for you and me, too.

After Jesus had been crucified and resurrected, He stayed on the Earth for forty days to teach the disciples about the Holy Ghost who was to come. **To whom also he shewed himself alive after his passion by many infallible proofs, being seen of them forty days, and speaking of the things pertaining to the kingdom of God** (Acts 1:3). Jesus was getting ready to leave the disciples, and He was doing everything He could to make the Holy Ghost as real to them as He possibly could before they received Him. He wanted them to understand that they could not do His work and take the Gospel to the world unless they received the Holy Ghost. Many people have tried to do that without the Holy Ghost, but they have failed.

During those forty days of jubilee, the Lord also proved that He had measured up to every claim He had made of Himself. The disciples knew that He was the real Christ, and they believed all that He taught and brought. They had failed somewhat before, but Jesus understood why; so He was getting them ready for the great coming of the Holy Spirit—the Spirit of truth. Jesus' last words before He left were, "Receive ye the Holy Ghost." **Then said Jesus to them again, Peace be unto you: as my Father hath sent me, even so send I you. And when he had said this, he breathed on them, and saith unto them, Receive ye the Holy Ghost** (John 20:21,22).

With the Holy Ghost in us, we have the Teacher with us wherever we go. When Jesus was here, the disciples could not have the Teacher with them wherever they went because they had to be where Jesus was. He had limited Himself to a tabernacle of clay like ours; but when Jesus had fulfilled His mission, He had to go away so the mission could continue. Jesus said, **I will never leave thee, nor forsake thee** (Hebrews 13:5).

THE SPIRIT IS WITH US

Through the Holy Spirit, we have Jesus with us all the time; and that is the Father's great plan—that each one of you has the person of the Holy Spirit living and dwelling on the inside of you to produce Heaven's fruit, to show you the right paths, to take you into the holiness of God. He teaches you what to do and what not to do. He teaches you what Heaven is like and what is expected of you so you can go there. He teaches you the Bible prophecies, what each one means and the reality of those prophecies—but only if you let Him give you that understanding.

The Holy Spirit will do for you what no other power can do and give you answers so you will not grope along as one in the night, but some Christians are in the night so much that they think the Christian life is awful; however, that is not the divine, Christian life. In the divine, Christian life, with the divine spiritual senses and with the physical senses made pure and clean like they were in Eden through the blood of the Lamb, you have what you need. There is no other foundation that can be laid. **For other foundation can no man lay than that is laid, which is Jesus Christ** (I Corinthians 3:11). There is no other name that can reach from the Cross to Heaven so the Lord can save your soul. You have divine greatness flowing to you, and you must learn to use it.

We all know that there are five human senses, but there are also the six divine senses that I just mentioned—hearing, sight, smell, taste, touch and faith—and the Holy Spirit knows how to use them in perfection. We know about our human senses because we are born with them. We understand the human ear more than we do the divine ear, and we understand human hearing more than divine hearing; but through the Spirit, I hear things that I would never be able to hear in the human sense.

They are so real that sometimes I do not know whether they are in the human or the spiritual realm; so I may turn and ask somebody, "Did you hear that?"

When you have all of this, you will be happy, but the devil does not want you to be happy; he wants you to be oppressed and depressed. He wants you to have misgivings about your salvation and about the truth for you. You may believe that somebody else has real salvation, but he does not want you to believe that you have it. You can believe that somebody else has the real Holy Ghost baptism as long as you do not believe you have it. The devil does not care how real the Spirit is to you when you are in church as long as you do not get anything out of the services or carry any of the great things of God away with you.

The devil seeks to rob people and make them feel like they are worthless or that they are outcasts. People tried to make Paul an outcast, but he refused to be one. He said, **I am crucified with Christ: nevertheless I live; yet not I, but Christ liveth in me** (Galatians 2:20). Paul delighted in Christ living on the inside of him, and you have to delight not only in Christ living in you but also in the person of the Holy Spirit living on the inside of you and making Himself real.

Again I say, the Holy Spirit is a person; so when are you going to start treating Him like one? He is the greatest person you will ever meet or have around you here on Earth. He is the most understanding and compassionate person, and He is with you to care for you in an even greater way than a mother is with her child.

You must be in harmony with the Spirit and agree with Him. The Bible says, **Can two walk together, except they be agreed** (Amos 3:3)?

NEVER OFFEND THE SPIRIT

And be not conformed to this world: but be ye transformed by the renewing of your mind, that ye may prove what is that good, and acceptable, and perfect, will of God (Romans 12:2). The Holy Ghost will not transform you if you are part of the world in any way; so if you are not living the victorious, Christian life, then you are stained with the world. It is influencing you, and you need to be transformed.

When you are transformed, you are brought into the newness of life that Jesus brought. The Bible tells us, **Having therefore, brethren, boldness to enter into the holiest by the blood of Jesus, By a new and living way** (Hebrews 10:19,20). Jesus brought the new and living way, but so many people have missed it and not enjoyed it because the Holy Ghost has to be right in the middle of it. When Jesus brought the new and living way, the Holy Ghost was included; and the Spirit will give you understanding of how to receive from the hand of the Lord as He takes you to the Holy Scriptures.

The Holy Spirit is so sensitive to any kind of spirit that is selfish, devilish or wrong. He is offended by sin of any kind, and He has come to bring judgments as well as victories; and He proved it by killing Ananias and Sapphira in the beginning of the Church. **But a certain man named Ananias, with Sapphira his wife, sold a possession, And kept back part of the price, his wife also being privy to it,**

and brought a certain part, and laid it at the apostles' feet. But Peter said, Ananias, why hath Satan filled thine heart to lie to the Holy Ghost, and to keep back part of the price of the land? Whiles it remained, was it not thine own? and after it was sold, was it not in thine own power? why hast thou conceived this thing in thine heart? thou hast not lied unto men, but unto God. And Ananias hearing these words fell down, and gave up the ghost: and great fear came on all them that heard these things. And the young men arose, wound him up, and carried him out, and buried him. And it was about the space of three hours after, when his wife, not knowing what was done, came in. And Peter answered unto her, Tell me whether ye sold the land for so much? And she said, Yea, for so much. Then Peter said unto her, How is it that ye have agreed together to tempt the Spirit of the Lord? behold, the feet of them which have buried thy husband are at the door, and shall carry thee out. Then fell she down straightway at his feet, and yielded up the ghost: and the

young men came in, and found her dead, and, carrying her forth, buried her by her husband. And great fear came upon all the church, and upon as many as heard these things (Acts 5:1–11).

You must not want the Holy Spirit to be angry with you any more than you want God to be angry with you. The Bible says, **It is a fearful thing to fall into the hands of the living God** (Hebrews 10:31). But people need to realize that it is also a terrible thing to fall into the hands of an angry Holy Spirit. He was angry with Ananias and his wife because they had brought sin into God's house, and He killed them.

THE GIFT OF DISCERNING

The Lord told me I would have to understand the spirit of man, the spirit of the devil and the Spirit of God and be able to separate those spirits; and the Spirit of truth brings the wonderful gift of the discerning of spirits. That gift is used only through certain people who are chosen by the Lord because He divides the gifts as He wills. **For to one is given by the Spirit the word of wisdom; to**

another the word of knowledge by the same Spirit; To another faith by the same Spirit; to another the gifts of healing by the same Spirit; To another the working of miracles; to another prophecy; to another discerning of spirits; to another divers kinds of tongues; to another the interpretation of tongues: But all these worketh that one and the selfsame Spirit, dividing to every man severally as he will (I Corinthians 12:8–11).

The gift of the Holy Ghost is for everybody, but the nine gifts of the Spirit are not. You may be as righteous and holy as God Himself, but God has to choose you for one or all of the nine gifts of the Spirit. I knew that, and I did not think God would ever choose me to receive even one of His gifts; but when I received the gift of the discerning of spirits, it seemed like everything turned into chaos. Some people are not conscious of the devil because they are not close enough to God to know that he really exists; but if you are not devil-conscious, you will not be God-conscious. I recognize the devil and his demons. I was taught there was a real devil from the time I was young, and I believed it. I did not have to get saved to believe there was a devil, and I never remember not believing there was a God.

HAVE NO FEAR

But the hour cometh, and now is, when the true worshippers shall worship the Father in spirit and in truth: for the Father seeketh such to worship him. God is a Spirit: and they that worship him must worship him in spirit and in truth (John 4:23,24). If you have the Spirit of truth, you will worship the Lord; and the Lord is always ready to be worshiped. He delights in being praised, and He delights in His faith working like He planned for it to in man. I am sure He delights in looking at those who are full of love and not those who are full of fear, frustration and distress. **There is no fear in love; but perfect love casteth out fear** (I John 4:18). There is no need to pray and pray to get rid of fear when the Spirit can flush it out so easily.

You must recognize the One who will take away all of your fear because He is the only one who can flow the love of God into your heart and mind until every speck of fear is gone. Do you think the Spirit wants to live with you in fear? Do you think He enjoys dining with you when you are trembling with fear? When you know you have victory over the devil, why do you worry about him? Just say, "Come on, Devil. I trampled you yesterday, and I have the same blood to use on you today; and I know it works."

You must not hinder the Spirit or try to improve on the truth because the truth cannot be improved on. The Lord never dresses up His truth; the devil is the one who does that kind of work because his works are counterfeit. The Lord puts the truth out just like it is. He speaks it, and it does not change; and a trillion years from now, it will still be the same. **The grass withereth, the flower fadeth: but the word of our God shall stand forever** (Isaiah 40:8). God spoke the Word, and He never changes. **For I am the LORD, I change not** (Malachi 3:6).

The Holy Spirit directs you into perfect obedience. If you have any imperfections in trying to obey God, it is because you are not completely giving over to the leadership of the Holy Spirit. When you can cry, "He leadeth me!" and mean it, the Spirit will direct you into the paths of humility and righteousness.

I challenge you to start a new life right now. Stop looking back and seeing that you were weak yesterday. Close the door on that weak day and on the times you failed to pray and fast when the Spirit bid you to. Close all the doors and start a new day—a day of the reality of the person of the Holy Ghost, the Spirit of Heaven's living truth.

Everything worthwhile is with us and ahead of us, and we must take hold of all of it. We must use it and step into the new and living way, walk in the holiness and righteousness of truth and give over to the Spirit of truth at all times. When He touches you with His gentle touch, let Him lead you where He wants you to go—into the prayer chamber, into fasting, into the Word or to help a lost soul find Jesus.

We live in the greatest hour that has ever been since Adam and Eve sinned against God and were cast out of Eden because Jesus brought the acceptable year of the Lord spoken of in Luke 4:19. It is the year of Jubilee, and we must live every day as a Jubilee day and every night as a Jubilee night. We have the tree of life to shelter us daily, and we have a blood hedge as Job had to protect us. Our lives are candles like Gideon's army had, and those who are full of the Holy Ghost are blowing the trumpets of praise daily and obeying the Word.

You who are baptized in the Holy Ghost must know who dwells within you. Has this chapter given you enough of an introduction through the Word and the Spirit of God that He has become a greater reality to you today? I sought God so faithfully for all of this so it would be just what you needed and so that you could understand the Holy Spirit as the Lord has given me understanding of Him.

CHAPTER **2**

The Spirit of Truth

Who is the Spirit of truth? We need to learn everything we can about what is in Him. People will talk about truth, but many of them do not really know the truth because they cannot know it without the Spirit of truth.

What is truth?—the Gospels. They are the truth that the Holy Spirit teaches us, and He will even tell us things about Jesus that are not recorded in the Gospels. There was not enough room in the Bible to include all the wonderful works the Lord performed as very man. Truth walked on Earth in a body of clay and brought great results through just one body. Now, the Spirit of truth walks in many bodies, and He is seeking to walk in many more bodies. Is the Spirit of truth walking with you? Does He talk when you talk and hear when you hear? Does the Spirit of truth work when you work?

The Spirit uses the Word of truth; so that means He uses Jesus, the Word made flesh. **And the Word was made flesh, and dwelt among us, (and we beheld his glory, the glory as of the only begotten of the Father,) full of grace and truth** (John 1:14). The Spirit uses the love and the goodness of Jesus. He uses the peace, the faith, the healing and the miracle power of Jesus.

ALWAYS GO BACK TO CALVARY

The Spirit of truth reveals Calvary in all of its power and glory, and Calvary will cleanse a person from all sin. It is the place where man receives dominion over all sin and justification from Heaven. We were once condemned, but no more. The Spirit of truth reveals the same righteousness and holy living that man had in Eden, and He reveals the fullness of the Godhead that is to dwell in the body of each individual. **For in him dwelleth all the fulness of the Godhead bodily** (Colossians 2:9). The fullness of the Godhead dwelt in Christ's body of clay, and He is our example. Every step He made shows us how to walk. Man had lost everything—his walk, his speech, his hearing—and Jesus came to buy it all back.

We have the six divine senses and the same divine faith that Jesus had when He lived in a house of clay like ours; and through His blood, we have become sons and daughters of God. All of the works of Jesus are being brought to us through the Spirit of truth; and they will enable us to talk like Him, to hear like Him and to see like Him.

Jesus came as a human being to be perfect in love, and He had love in perfection. In the Sermon on the Mount, He said, **Be ye therefore perfect, even as your Father which is in heaven is perfect** (Matthew 5:48). Jesus came to show people how that could be done because He had taken on the fashion of a man with all of the same weaknesses that man has.

Jesus keeps taking us back to Calvary in song, in praise and in word. He can never teach anyone all of Calvary because it is so great and mammoth. Sinai was a wonderful experience for the Israelite people even though they did not accept it as such; but Calvary is much greater than Sinai, and yet there are so few people who have really accepted it. Mount Calvary is the highest mountain that will ever be in the lives of human beings. It reaches all the way to God's throne in Heaven, and everybody can find Heaven through Calvary if they are led by the Spirit.

NO HELP OUTSIDE OF TRUTH

The Holy Spirit will only fellowship with you in truth, and it has to be the whole truth because He will back away if there is anything false in you. He will give you a chance to get rid of it; but if you do not, He will leave. You have to be for real, but you can only be for real through truth. If you are outside the truth, you are a counterfeit before God.

Many people pray outside of truth, but you have to pray in the truth and according to the will of God for every prayer to be heard. When you do not know how to pray for something, either the Holy Spirit or Jesus will make intercession for you according to the will of God. **And he that searcheth the hearts knoweth what is the mind of the Spirit, because he maketh intercession for the saints according to the will of God** (Romans 8:27). **It is Christ that died, yea rather, that is risen again, who is even at the right hand of God, who also maketh intercession for us** (Romans 8:34).

And grieve not the holy Spirit of God, whereby ye are sealed unto the day of redemption (Ephesians 4:30). Every time you grieve the Spirit, it makes you weak; and those weaknesses finally add up until you are too weak to overcome. If you grieve Him too much, He will leave you. Then the enemy gets in, and the Holy Spirit no longer has your mind; and He has to work through the mind to baptize and teach you.

When you do not accept the promises of God in truth, the Spirit of truth is grieved and disappointed. When you do not use the truth in total obedience, the promises cannot be fulfilled; and then you wonder, "Why doesn't God keep His promises?"—because He made every promise through truth, and they can only be fulfilled through truth. The Spirit of truth is with us to help us know what truth really is so there will be no mistake.

Jesus said, **And ye shall know the truth, and the truth shall make you free** (John 8:32). You have to know what truth is before you can be free. When you know the Spirit of truth, you will know the Son of God. When you know the Son, you will know the Father; and when you know the Trinity, you will be free.

You had to know the truth about God's promise of salvation before you started for Calvary in order to receive it. Then the Holy Spirit helped you by giving you a measure of faith that took you to Calvary, and only through truth can you keep your eyes on Calvary.

And the LORD sent fiery serpents among the people, and they bit the people; and much people of Israel died. And the LORD said unto Moses, Make thee a fiery serpent, and set it upon a pole: and it shall come to pass, that every one that is bitten, when he looketh upon it, shall live (Numbers 21:6,8).

God told Moses to tell the people to look at the serpent of brass on the tree, a symbol of the cursed condition of Christ on the Cross. You have to look, and then only through truth can you keep on looking.

SAVED BY TRUTH

If you do not know the truth, how can the Spirit of truth work? The truth has to be in you for it to work; it cannot be outside of you, around you or in book form in your hand. The Holy Spirit uses what is inside of us, and our souls are a reservoir. There is no limit to the capacity of the soul because it came from God. It can hold the whole Godhead and all of Heaven.

The truth is for the sinner. **If we confess our sins, he is faithful and just to forgive us our sins, and to cleanse us from all unrighteousness** (I John 1:9). The Lord will not leave one tiny particle of sin. The Spirit works in perfection with truth, and He works in perfection with a soul to redeem it.

That if thou shalt confess with thy mouth the Lord Jesus, and shalt believe in thine heart that God hath raised him from the

dead, thou shalt be saved (Romans 10:9). When you confess the Lord Jesus, you are confessing all the truth that He brought; then you have to believe it. Salvation is not outside of you; and it does not come by shaking the preacher's hand, joining a church or being baptized in water. Salvation is of the heart.

Only perfect truth is used in salvation, perfect truth that your sins will be cast into the sea of forgetfulness and never again be remembered against you. **He will have compassion upon us; he will subdue our iniquities; and thou wilt cast all their sins into the depths of the sea** (Micah 7:19). When your sins are gone, you are to live pure, clean and holy every day because Jesus came and made it possible.

Nothing can be mixed in with the perfect truth—not your thoughts or opinions, your weaknesses or what somebody else thinks. Truth has to be pure because it is no good if it is contaminated. It is no longer the truth of God because you have allowed it to be ruined. Your spirit contaminated it, so you have rendered the truth helpless; and it will not stay.

Only the perfect truth brings perfect results from God. Jesus said, **For John truly baptized with water; but ye shall be baptized with the Holy Ghost** (Acts 1:5). You can be baptized in the Spirit of truth, but there can be nothing false or sinful in your heart. All untruths have to go before the Spirit of truth will baptize you.

Now ye are clean through the word [through the truth] **which I have spoken unto you** (John 15:3). Jesus was truth, and only through the truth can you be made clean. The greatness of truth washed away your sins and made you a new creature. **Therefore if any man be in Christ, he is a new creature: old things are passed away; behold, all things are become new** (II Corinthians 5:17). That is why it is essential that you know the truth, but how well do you know Jesus? You do not know any more about Him than the reality you have in Him today. He gave you nothing but the truth; and in that truth, you have all you need to use from the cradle to the grave... or until Rapture day!

Jesus said, **I am the way, the truth, and the**

life: no man cometh unto the Father, but by me (John 14:6); so you never have to look beyond Jesus. He is the source of all truth for the human race, and He never changes. **Jesus Christ the same yesterday, and today, and forever** (Hebrews 13:8).

Jesus was not only truth; He was a testimony to truth and to righteous, holy living. The Bible says there was no guile to be found in His mouth. **Who did no sin, neither was guile found in his mouth** (I Peter 2:22). The Holy Spirit will give you the right Jesus attitude, and you will find the attitude of Jesus toward so many things in the Sermon on the Mount.

Jesus is the Second Adam who destroyed all the false for us and bought us back with truth. The first Adam, the father of the human race, sold us all into bondage when he sold everything to the devil for just a handful of ashes; but Jesus came to save us from all of that. **For the Son of man is come to seek and to save that which was lost** (Luke 19:10). This does not say that which *is* lost but that which *was* lost.

Such darkness was upon the Earth when

Jesus came because there was no truth of deliverance from all sin, no truth of holy living, no truth of the six divine senses or of walking in love in perfection and in the perfect will of God; but the Spirit of truth will guide you into all truth. **Howbeit when he, the Spirit of truth, is come, he will guide you into all truth: for he shall not speak of himself; but whatsoever he shall hear** [from the Father and the Son]**, that shall he speak: and he will shew you things to come. He shall glorify me: for he shall receive of mine, and shall shew it unto you** (John 16:13,14). The Holy Spirit will show you what?—the truth concerning Jesus. He will receive what Jesus has with the Father today and show it unto us. You have to let the Spirit guide you into *all truth*; and there is no excuse for us to be in anything false, especially concerning the Holy Ghost.

Truth never makes an error, and it always gives the right answer; but some of you will not let the Holy Spirit work through you. He is the one who will work the truth in you until everything that hinders you and everything the devil comes against you with are destroyed, but you have to put those things into His hands.

THE SPIRIT MAKES GOD REAL

Blessed are the pure in heart: for they shall see God (Matthew 5:8). We don't have to wait until we are in Heaven to see God; we are to see God now in Jesus and in all the works of the Holy Spirit. In Heaven, we will behold God with our eyes and look upon His face; but until then, we can see His hand moving through His works, His great love and the results of His wonderful, divine blood. We can see the high arm of God that is spoken of in the Bible. **Thou hast a mighty arm: strong is thy hand, and high is thy right hand** (Psalm 89:13). **The God of this people of Israel chose our fathers, and exalted the people when they dwelt as strangers in the land of Egypt, and with an high arm brought he them out of it** (Acts 13:17).

The Holy Spirit is as necessary to our spiritual life as air is to our physical life. If your air was cut off right now, you would die; and without the Spirit of truth helping us in this life, we would be dead. The Holy Spirit plays such a great part in getting to a person's soul before he is saved and then working with that soul at the time he is saved and after he is saved; yet what kind of treatment does He receive at the hands of men today? It is awful how He is criticized and made fun of. People mock His miracles and healings, the truth and His works; and they despise Pentecost. I don't want man's Pentecost, but I am proud of God's Pentecost because it is the pure truth.

How do you treat the Holy Spirit? He moves inside of you to begin His great ministration, working from within to do the work that needs to be done outside; but He can only do His mighty works as you yield yourself to Him.

THE SPIRIT BRINGS MIRACLES

Some of you have the Holy Ghost, but you do not yield to Him so He can release the faith of God within you. I yield to Him, and you have to learn to do it, too. Then you can pray for yourself and for others and get results. The reason it takes some of you a long time to get your miracles is because you do not yield to the Holy Ghost. You have Him, but you don't yield to Him; and you want somebody else to pray the prayer of faith for you. When you pray for yourself and get results, it strengthens your faith.

My mother used to say, "I never ask anybody to pray for me when I get sick until I have prayed for myself." I have never forgotten that. Neither have I ever heard anybody else say, "Honey, you had better get up your faith; the devil is going to try you." I was just a little youngster in grade school; but I knew that meant that Mama would pray, and I would be well the next morning. If I had a high fever, it would leave me; and I knew it would.

How yielded are you to the Holy Ghost? Do you plan to stay sick or do you plan to get well? Do you meet the conditions of the promises of God? Jesus said, **And these signs shall follow them that believe; In my name shall they cast out devils...they shall lay hands on the sick, and they shall recover** (Mark 16:17,18). When the Lord healed people, He healed them of everything.

God's miracles are given in such simplicity, but He wants us to be conscious of where they come from. The doctor may tell you that you have only a little while to live, and you will think that is a definite thing. I believe in good doctors, good nurses and good hospitals, and good medical people sponsor my ministry and belong to my church; but when they have done all they can do, the Lord is ready to do the rest in such a simple manner.

After the Lord had brought me back from the edge of the grave and made me whole, He told me, "You will go on a long fast." I did go on that fast; and after it was over, I was never the same. I died to everything of the world saying, "I'll do whatever you want, God, no matter what it is. I want your divine will." At that time was when the Lord gave me His gift for the healing of the people, and I could hardly wait to get to the next crusade to use that wonderful gift that the Lord had given to me.

The first miracle I remember was for a woman on crutches. She hobbled up before me; and when I laid hands on her, I knew she would walk. Her crutches fell to the floor, and she walked like she had never been crippled. Then she left her crutches in the building for the rest of the crusade so that all could see that she was free.

In my next crusade, a daddy brought his baby who was born with one side of its face deformed. There were so many people crowded into the building that day, and that man stood holding his baby in the healing line for I don't know how long because he was determined to get a miracle.

When the man finally got to me, I just felt like taking the baby into my arms. As I prayed, I was looking at its little face—one side beautiful and the other side deformed—and it was like a gentle breeze came over it; and the baby was instantly made whole. In this last hour, God is going to do the unthinkable and the unbelievable; *and only through the Holy Spirit will we be able to believe enough, saith the Lord.*

You cannot give up. That daddy was determined to receive a miracle just like the men were in the Bible who had carried the man with palsy to Jesus. When they arrived, they could not get into the house; so they removed part of the roof and let the man down to

Jesus...and Jesus healed him.

And they come unto him [Jesus], **bringing one sick of the palsy, which was borne of four. And when they could not come nigh unto him for the press, they uncovered the roof where he was: and when they had broken it up, they let down the bed wherein the sick of the palsy lay...(he saith to the sick of the palsy,) I say unto thee, Arise, and take up thy bed, and go thy way into thine house. And immediately he arose, took up the bed, and went forth before them all; insomuch that they were all amazed, and glorified God, saying, We never saw it on this fashion** (Mark 2:3,4,10–12).

THE WATER OF LIFE

This is he that came by water and blood, even Jesus Christ; not by water only, but by water and blood. And it is the Spirit that beareth witness, because the Spirit is truth (I John 5:6). The Spirit is truth, and there is no truth without the Spirit of God.

For there are three that bear record in heaven, the Father, the Word [Jesus], **and the Holy Ghost: and these three are one**

(I John 5:7). The Father, the Son and the Holy Ghost are three separate personalities; but they are one. **And there are three that bear witness in earth, the Spirit, and the water, and the blood: and these three agree in one** (I John 5:8). This means that the Spirit of truth, the water of life and the divine blood agree in one.

Many people have not understood this and have said that the water mentioned in that verse was referring to the physical birth. Jesus did not come talking about physical birth; He came as the water of life, so this water is life water. It is not Earth's water that we drink either because you know that our natural water does not bear witness of the spiritual greatness of God. Spiritual things have to be spiritually discerned, so this is the spiritual water of life that bears witness.

Jesus told the Samaritan woman at the well that He would give her water so that she would never thirst again. **Jesus…said unto her, Whosoever drinketh of this water shall thirst again: But whosoever drinketh of the water that I shall give him shall never**

thirst; but the water that I shall give him shall be in him a well of water springing up into everlasting life (John 4:13,14). As Jesus talked to her, He took her from the water that she had come to draw to the spiritual water. Earth's water did not bear witness to the woman; it was the spiritual water she had received that went into action to bear witness. Then she ran into the city with what Jesus had told her, and she started a revival. **The woman then left her waterpot, and went her way into the city, and saith to the men, Come, see a man, which told me all things that ever I did: is not this the Christ** (John 4:28,29)?

It is that same spiritual water that bears witness to us. Then the blood and the Spirit of truth bear witness through us, not the spirit of man. Again, I say that these three agree in one, but the spirit of man certainly would disagree.

THE DIVINE BLOOD

The blood mentioned in I John 5:8 is not physical blood; it is the divine blood that is needed for cleansing. There are different types of human blood, but there is only one type of divine blood—holy blood that gives life for all eternity. It had so much life in it that it gave Adam and Eve enough life in a body of clay to live forever and never be sick; but when they lost that divine blood, sickness took over.

We were not born with divine blood, so sickness can afflict our bodies; and we have to fight it off through divine blood. We receive healings for the body through divine blood; and the Bible says that with the Lord's blood stripes, we are healed. **But he was wounded for our transgressions, he was bruised for our iniquities: the chastisement of our peace was upon him; and with his stripes we are healed** (Isaiah 53:5).

The divine blood that the Lord put in the bodies of Adam and Eve was to have kept all weakness, sickness, death and anything unlike God away from their bodies; and they never would have aged. Even after 6000 years, their teeth would have been just as good as ever. Adam and Eve were to have had nothing but pure truth and to have always had pure life, pure love and pure grace; and they did live in pure truth while they were in Eden.

Everything is pure in pure truth.

Without divine blood for the body, man can only live such a short time; but that divine blood has extended life for many people. Death was at their door; but the healing or miracle came as the divine blood flowed, and it gave them good health.

MANNA FROM ON HIGH

This glorious Holy Spirit ministration means depending on Jesus 100 percent and depending on the Spirit of truth to serve you everything that Jesus brought. Stop going to the pauper's table. God spread a table for the Israelites in the wilderness that was full of food they could see and eat, and it was manna from Heaven. **And the manna was as coriander seed, and the colour thereof as the colour of bdellium. And the people went about, and gathered it, and ground it in mills, or beat it in a mortar, and baked it in pans, and made cakes of it: and the taste of it was as the taste of fresh oil. And when the dew fell upon the camp in the night, the manna fell upon it** (Numbers 11:7–9).

We are being fed manna from Heaven today,

but we do not have to go out and gather it six days a week as the Israelites had to. We have the heavenly manna to eat and dwell on all the time. The Lord said, **I am that bread of life. Your fathers did eat manna in the wilderness, and are dead. This is the bread which cometh down from heaven, that a man may eat thereof, and not die. I am the living bread which came down from heaven: if any man eat of this bread, he shall live forever: and the bread that I will give is my flesh, which I will give for the life of the world** (John 6:48–51).

Jesus went on to say that, spiritually speaking, we have to eat the manna from Heaven, which is His flesh, and drink His blood, which is the divine blood of power that will be within us. **Then Jesus said unto them, Verily, verily, I say unto you, Except ye eat the flesh of the Son of man, and drink his blood, ye have no life in you. Whoso eateth my flesh, and drinketh my blood, hath eternal life; and I will raise him up at the last day. For my flesh is meat indeed, and my blood is drink indeed. He that eateth my**

flesh, and drinketh my blood, dwelleth in me, and I in him. As the living Father hath sent me, and I live by the Father: so he that eateth me, even he shall live by me. This is that bread which came down from heaven: not as your fathers did eat manna, and are dead: he that eateth of this bread shall live forever (John 6:53–58).

THE HOLY SPIRIT PRODUCES FAITH

The Lord serves the fruit of faith to you as a free gift. Then the Lord produces in you the faith He must use through you to defeat the powers of the devil and to trample devils underfoot. **Behold, I give unto you power to tread on serpents and scorpions, and over all the power of the enemy** (Luke 10:19).

Submit yourselves therefore to God. Resist the devil, and he will flee from you (James 4:7). God gives you the faith to put the devil to flight, but that fruit must be produced inside a pure soul because the Spirit of truth can work with only that which is pure. He grows the fruit of faith and produces it in any amount you need. He has no trouble producing the fruits of the Spirit in you unless you give Him trouble.

The Spirit of truth is also the Spirit of divine faith, and He makes the promises of God become living reality. The Bible says we are to contend for the faith that was once delivered to the saints. **Beloved, when I gave all diligence to write unto you of the common salvation, it was needful for me to write unto you, and exhort you that ye should earnestly contend for the faith which was once delivered unto the saints** (Jude 1:3). Contend means to struggle and fight for something, and you have to do that any time you use God's great faith. As you struggle against the enemy, he will fight you in every way he can when you use the fantastic faith that was delivered to the saints; but they too had to fight and struggle for it.

Abraham had that faith, but he had to struggle and fight for it to do what God wanted done. He had to take his son to Mount Moriah and offer him as a sacrifice unto God even though his whole heart was in Isaac, but thank God, he loved God more.

THE SPIRIT SERVES LOVE

The Holy Spirit serves divine love. He grows that fruit of love inside you and then serves it through you, and the Bible says that it multiplies. He served the divine Word through the Christians in the beginning of the Church and it multiplied, increased and prevailed. **But the word of God grew and multiplied** (Acts 12:24). **And the word of God increased** (Acts 6:7). **So mightily grew the word of God and prevailed** (Acts 19:20).

When the Holy Spirit can serve the Word through you, it brings wonderful, glorious results; but when you serve it within your own spirit and with your own little opinions, it does not do much. Then you think, "I used the Word, but it didn't work." Try giving yourself over to the Spirit and letting Him use the Word through you with the great love that He produces inside of you.

Paul had that love; and he said, **That ye, being rooted and grounded in love, May be able to comprehend with all saints what is the breadth, and length, and depth, and height; And to know the love of Christ,**

which passeth knowledge (Ephesians 3:17–19). No human being can measure divine love or comprehend the greatness of it without the Spirit of truth. He is the only one who can let you know what is real about the great love of God.

The Spirit served Paul so much love because he reached for it to serve it to others. You cannot be selfish with the Holy Spirit. You must reach for divine love, not to cuddle up in it yourself but to serve it; and as you serve that love, you will have plenty more. All the warmth and grace of it will be yours because you cannot handle God's love without receiving the benefits, the strength and the greatness of it.

When you serve God's love, you serve His strength; but how can you serve God's strength without your share being there, too? When you are helping to serve others, you are being served, too—God and the Holy Spirit see to that.

The Holy Spirit cannot serve you any of the fruits of the Spirit unless they are within you, not without. He has that authority from

Heaven to serve that which is within, but you have to be yielded to Him. You have the choice of letting Him serve you or not serve you, but you cannot resist Him and still expect Him to serve you. You must yield to Him so the truth can be produced in Heaven's perfection.

THE SPIRIT WORKS FOR US

With the Holy Ghost, we go from grace to grace truth, grace to grace love, grace to grace faith, grace to grace hope, grace to grace courage and grace to grace determination. **And of his fulness have all we received, and grace for grace** (John 1:16). Jesus brought everything we need, and you can find it all in the one word "grace," which is all the divine favor of God for us. Adam and Eve had it and lost it, so Jesus came and bought it back and offered it to everyone.

The Holy Spirit will look out for you as you look out for a lost world. Those who will work with the vision of truth to take Jesus to the whole world are the ones who are really going to enjoy the glorious way of life in abundance on the inside of them. Jesus said, **And this gospel of the kingdom shall be**

preached in all the world for a witness unto all nations; and then shall the end come (Matthew 24:14).

Our God is wonderful, and this is a glorious day for everyone who will let it be—glorious for miracles and healings and for a clear mind. It is glorious to know that you have the Holy Spirit Himself living and dwelling inside, the One who is ready to take your burdens and your mind battles. Become conscious of the person of the Holy Spirit and let Him become real to you so you can work with Him in love and faith in perfection. That will bring joy in perfection, and joy brings strength in perfection.

The Holy Spirit will show you how to make each step that Jesus made. He will not just tell you how; He will go with you wherever you go and help you to make each step. He will not just tell you what Jesus might have said; He will give you exactly what Jesus would say in whatever situation you are in. If you give somebody wisdom and knowledge about a situation, you must make sure those things come from On High and not from you.

The Lord said that if you would seek Him with your whole heart, you would find Him; and that is a Spirit of truth promise. **And ye shall seek me, and find me, when ye shall search for me with all your heart** (Jeremiah 29:13).

It is so simple for you to give your mind to the Spirit when you learn how. All members of the bridal company must learn how to turn their minds over to the Spirit. He can erase every problem in a moment when you give Him complete control. Then He can take over your mind and use it as His very own. You will know the very thoughts of God and the very thoughts of the Spirit of truth, and those are the thoughts we need. We must have direct communion and direct fellowship with divinity.

CHAPTER 3

30 Bible Reasons
Why You Must Have the Holy Ghost to Make the Rapture

Now that you have had an introduction to the person of the Holy Spirit, it is important for you to know from the Bible why you have to have Him living inside you; and this chapter will give you thirty reasons straight from the Word of God. When I say the Bible teaches that you must have the Holy Ghost baptism to make the Rapture, some think I mean that no one can go to Heaven without the Holy Ghost; but that is not so. A person who is born of the Spirit of God will go to Heaven when he or she dies. All it takes to go to Heaven is a born-again experience through the blood of Christ; however, more power will be required for us to go to Heaven by way of the Rapture than by way of the grave. We who are alive on the face of the Earth when Jesus comes will need something extra—we will need the Holy Ghost baptism before we can be caught up to meet the Lord in the air, and the Bible makes that very plain.

REASON ONE:
ONLY THE HOLY GHOST'S POWER WITHIN WILL CHANGE YOU.

Now unto him that is able to do exceeding abundantly above all that we ask or think, according to the power that worketh in us (Ephesians 3:20). This scripture says *according to the power that worketh in us.* It is impossible for the power of God to work in you with great force unless you have the Holy Ghost baptism. **But ye shall receive power, after that the Holy Ghost is come upon you** (Acts 1:8). **For he** [the Holy Ghost] **dwelleth *with* you, and shall be *in* you** (John 14:17). The Bible clearly makes the distinction between the Holy Ghost being *with* a Christian and the Holy Ghost being *in* a Christian. The

Holy Ghost *in* a person is what will change him or her at the time of the Rapture.

REASON TWO:
ONLY OBEDIENT HEARTS WILL BE TAKEN IN THE RAPTURE.

And we are his witnesses of these things; and so is also the Holy Ghost, whom God hath given to them that obey him (Acts 5:32). God promised He would give the Holy Ghost to those who obey Him, and you are being disobedient when you fail to accept His promise. **For the promise is unto you, and to your children, and to all that are afar off, even as many as the Lord our God shall call** (Acts 2:39). The obedient will seek until they receive the Holy Ghost.

REASON THREE:
ANYONE WHO LIMITS GOD WILL NEVER RECEIVE HIS BEST.

Yea, they turned back and tempted God, and limited the Holy One of Israel (Psalm 78:41). Israel doubted God; and because of her unbelief, she limited God and could not go into the land of Canaan for forty years. If you doubt God, you will fail to make the Rapture because those who are taken will not limit God with unbelief. Anyone who limits God will never receive His best, and to be caught up to meet the Lord in the air and escape the Tribulation Period is certainly God's best.

REASON FOUR:

THEY RECEIVED THE HOLY GHOST AND SPOKE IN TONGUES DURING THE EARLY RAIN.

Be patient therefore, brethren, unto the coming of the Lord. Behold, the husbandman waiteth for the precious fruit of the earth, and hath long patience for it, until he receive the early and latter rain (James 5:7). And the Early Rain did fall at Pentecost. The prophet Joel looked down through the eyes of the Holy Ghost and saw this hour and said, **And it shall come to pass afterward, that I will pour out my spirit upon all flesh** (Joel 2:28). It continued to fall during the Early Church period; and during that time, every gift and fruit of the Spirit were manifested in the Church until the nine gifts and the nine fruits of the Spirit hung as eighteen perfect apples upon a perfect tree. The Early Church is our example for today, and the disciples in that Church had the Holy Ghost baptism with the evidence of speaking with other tongues.

REASON FIVE:
YOU MUST RECEIVE THE HOLY GHOST AND SPEAK IN TONGUES DURING THIS LATTER RAIN.

During the Early Church period, the Holy Ghost had control and performed mighty miracles in the midst of the people; but then the devil wormed his way into the Church, and she lost her power. **That which the palmerworm hath left hath the locust eaten; and that which the locust hath left hath the cankerworm eaten; and that which the cankerworm hath left hath the caterpillar eaten** (Joel 1:4). Joel prophesied that this would happen to the Church, and it did. Since then, God has waited with long patience for almost 2000 years for the harvest of the Latter Rain. **And I will restore to you the years that the locust hath eaten, the cankerworm, and the caterpillar, and the palmerworm, my great army which I sent among you** (Joel 2:25).

The Lord said He would restore the power

to the Church in the last days; and now, that power is here. The Latter Rain is the power of the Holy Ghost, and you cannot be ready for the Lord's coming without this power. The Bible says that just before the coming of the Son of God, the Holy Ghost will be poured out—not a sprinkle but a downpour of the Spirit. Why do you think He promised to pour out His Spirit on us in the last days if it was not going to be needed in our preparation for His coming? Jesus said, **I will pour out in those days of my Spirit** (Acts 2:18). Whatever keeps you from receiving the Holy Ghost in this age of the downpour of the Spirit will certainly keep you out of the Rapture. No one can be caught up in the Rapture without first receiving the Holy Ghost baptism.

REASON SIX:
SPEAKING IN TONGUES IS A SIGN THAT FOLLOWS BELIEVERS.

And these signs shall follow them that believe...they shall speak with new tongues (Mark 16:17). Believers will speak with a new tongue, not with the converted tongue that some claim when they want to deny the real baptism of the Spirit. Others say we are to take it by faith, but that would mean there is no Holy Ghost for you. Those people just give mental assent to the baptism and then think no more about it, but the devil is the one who spews out all of those lies. If people are true Bible believers, they will receive the Holy Ghost.

For what if some did not believe? shall their unbelief make the faith of God without effect? God forbid: yea, let God be true, but every man a liar; as it is written, That thou mightest be justified in thy sayings, and mightest overcome when thou art judged (Romans 3:3,4). The faith of God surely includes yielding to the Holy Ghost, and you must believe the Word of God over the theories of man. Teachings against the Holy Ghost baptism are in conflict with the Word of God which states that tongues is one of the signs that shall follow believers.

REASON SEVEN:
YOU MUST BE AN OVERCOMER.

Jesus received the Holy Ghost when He was here, and John the Baptist saw the Spirit descend on Him. **And he saw the Spirit of God descending like a dove, and lighting upon him** (Matthew 3:16). The Bible also says, **God anointed Jesus of Nazareth with the Holy Ghost and with power** (Acts 10:38). That power makes us overcomers.

Because thou hast kept the word of my patience, I also will keep thee from the hour of temptation, which shall come upon all the world, to try them that dwell upon the earth. Behold, I come quickly: hold that fast which thou hast, that no man take thy crown. Him that overcometh will I make a pillar in the temple of my God (Revelation 3:10–12). God considered it necessary for Jesus to have the Holy Ghost, and it is vital that you too have that power within you if you are to be an overcomer for the Lord. Only the overcomers will be taken when Jesus returns.

REASON EIGHT:

JESUS IS COMING AFTER A CHURCH WITHOUT SPOT OR WRINKLE.

That he might present it to himself a glorious church, not having spot, or wrinkle, or any such thing; but that it should be holy

and without blemish (Ephesians 5:27). Only the Holy Ghost can get the spots and wrinkles out. **Who is she that looketh forth as the morning, fair as the moon, clear as the sun, and terrible as an army with banners** (Song of Solomon 6:10)? This is speaking of the Bride of Christ, a Bride without blemish who is fair and beautiful to behold. It will take the Holy Ghost to give the Church the power to conquer and the purity to be rid of all spots and wrinkles.

REASON NINE:
JESUS IS COMING FOR THOSE WHO ARE ALIVE IN HIS SPIRIT.

I know thy works, that thou art neither cold nor hot: I would thou wert cold or hot. So then because thou art lukewarm, and neither cold nor hot, I will spue thee out of my mouth (Revelation 3:15,16). Some people claim that all Christians will make the Rapture, but this verse tells us that lukewarm Christians will be spewed out of God's mouth. This is not speaking of sinners because sinners cannot be in the mouth of God; but lukewarm Christians are ones who have been in

Christ or He could not spew them out of His mouth. Lukewarm Christian, God will spew you into the Tribulation Period.

Awake thou that sleepest, and arise from the dead, and Christ shall give thee light. See then that ye walk circumspectly, not as fools, but as wise, Redeeming the time, because the days are evil (Ephesians 5:14–16). Those who will be taken in the Rapture will be alive in the Lord's Spirit as they await His coming.

REASON TEN:
YOU MUST HAVE OIL IN YOUR LAMP.

Then shall the kingdom of heaven be likened unto ten virgins, which took their lamps, and went forth to meet the bridegroom. And five of them were wise, and five were foolish (Matthew 25:1,2). Jesus called them virgins, which means they were ten pure souls; but five of them were foolish. You can have Jesus in your heart and still be a foolish soul by not letting Him lead you on into the deepness of the Spirit and by not doing what He tells you to do.

They that were foolish took their lamps,

and took no oil with them: But the wise took oil in their vessels with their lamps (Matthew 25:3,4). The oil mentioned in those scriptures signifies the Holy Ghost—five had the oil of the Holy Ghost and five did not. The foolish virgins had some of the Spirit of the Lord, but they did not have the oil of the Holy Ghost that the wise had. **While the bridegroom tarried, they all slumbered and slept. And at midnight there was a cry made, Behold, the bridegroom cometh; go ye out to meet him. Then all those virgins arose, and trimmed their lamps. And the foolish said unto the wise, Give us of your oil; for our lamps are gone out. But the wise answered, saying, Not so; lest there be not enough for us and you: but go ye rather to them that sell, and buy for yourselves. And while they went to buy, the bridegroom came; and they that were ready went in with him to the marriage: and the door was shut. Afterward came also the other virgins, saying, Lord, Lord, open to us. But he answered and said, Verily I say unto you, I know you not** (Matthew 25:5–12).

After the bridegroom had come, the foolish virgins tried to get the oil so that they would be accepted; but it was too late. Jesus was saying to them, "You are not a part of my Bride, and I don't know you. You must go into the Tribulation Period." Without the oil of the Holy Spirit, you will not be taken in the Rapture. **Watch therefore, for ye know neither the day nor the hour wherein the Son of man cometh** (Matthew 25:13).

REASON ELEVEN:
THE RAPTURED SAINTS WILL ESCAPE DEATH.

We are getting close to the Rapture, and it is going to be the Holy Ghost working within us who will change us in the twinkling of an eye. **Behold, I shew you a mystery; We shall not all sleep, but we shall all be changed, In a moment, in the twinkling of an eye, at the last trump: for the trumpet shall sound, and the dead shall be raised incorruptible, and we shall be changed** (I Corinthians 15:51,52). This change is not death because death will not have a chance to touch those who are taken in the Rapture. The Holy Ghost who works within you will change you.

On the other hand, Hebrews tells us, **It is appointed unto men once to die, but after this the judgment** (Hebrews 9:27). Remember, there is an appointment of death to every man, but I Corinthians tells us that some will escape this appointment. How can this be done?—by finding favor in the eyes of God through yielding completely to the Holy Ghost.

REASON TWELVE:
THE RAPTURE CAN BE SEEN IN OLD TESTAMENT TYPES AND SHADOWS.

In the Old Testament, we find types and shadows of the Rapture. **And Enoch walked with God: and he was not; for God took him** (Genesis 5:24). Enoch found favor with God and was caught up to Heaven. His family did not go up with him; they had to go the way of the grave. This does not mean they were lost; it means that it takes greater favor with God to go to Heaven alive than it does to go the way of the grave.

Elijah, like Enoch, is also a type of the raptured Christian. The Bible tells us in II Kings 2:11 that he was caught up while others who loved God were left behind. They did not all go to hell; they simply did not find the favor with God that it would have taken for them to be caught up. Elisha did not have the miracle power when Elijah was taken, and he was left. Elisha is a type of the Christian who will be left when Jesus comes because again I say that it takes more power to be raptured than it does to go the way of the grave.

In Genesis 24, we find another beautiful picture of a type and shadow of the Rapture which we have already studied in Chapter One. In it, Abraham is a type of God; and Abraham's servant is a type of the Holy Ghost. Isaac is a type of Christ, and Rebekah is a type of the Bride of Christ. When Abraham sent his servant into another country to find a bride for Isaac, he did not return with Rebekah's whole family; he brought back only Rebekah. In the same way, God has sent the Holy Ghost into this world to find a Bride for His Son, Jesus. It takes something very special to be caught away with the Lord; and in our day, it will take the Holy Ghost baptism.

REASON THIRTEEN:
YOU MUST BE COUNTED WORTHY TO ESCAPE.

Not everybody will make the Rapture, and many will go into the Tribulation Period. **And when he had opened the fifth seal, I saw under the altar the souls of them that were slain for the word of God, and for the testimony which they held: And they cried with a loud voice, saying, How long, O Lord, holy and true, dost thou not judge and avenge our blood on them that dwell on the earth? And white robes were given unto every one of them; and it was said unto them, that they should rest yet for a little season, until their fellow servants also and their brethren, that should be killed as they were, should be fulfilled** (Revelation 6:9–11). The end of this verse is talking about Christians who will be left behind in the Tribulation Period.

Watch ye therefore, and pray always, that ye may be accounted worthy to escape all these things that shall come to pass, and to stand before the Son of man (Luke 21:36). This scripture plainly tells us that only those who are counted worthy will be caught up. Jesus will come as a thief in the night and gather up His jewels. **For yourselves know perfectly that the day of the Lord so cometh as a thief in the night** (I Thessalonians 5:2).

How do you expect to have the sparkle the Lord requires without the Holy Ghost? **Thou hast a few names even in Sardis which have not defiled their garments; and they shall walk with me in white: for they are worthy** (Revelation 3:4). Notice that they were worthy. This is a Holy Ghost dispensation, and everyone who wants to can receive the Holy Ghost; so how can you be counted worthy in the eyes of God when you are rejecting His power for service? Stephen told the people, **Ye stiffnecked and uncircumcised in heart and ears, ye do always resist the Holy Ghost** (Acts 7:51). Timothy described the world church today as **having a form of godliness, but denying the power thereof: from such turn away** (II Timothy 3:5). When you reject the Holy Ghost, you are refusing His power.

The dead churches of today don't have the

Holy Spirit; they have only the spirit of flesh and the spirit of the world. They have only a form of godliness; but we have living reality in the Holy Ghost, the One who operates the spiritual Church. We also have living reality in the promises of God that the Spirit is our guide and our shelter in time of storm. He is our love in perfection, and He knows what we need. He teaches us how to pray, and He helps us to believe to receive. He helps us not only to become holy but to stay holy in all truth with no errors. He never makes a mistake because He is divinity.

REASON FOURTEEN:
THE MAN CHILD OF REVELATION WILL BE TAKEN.

The woman mentioned in Revelation 12 is Israel, and the man child is the 144,000 Jews who are spoken of again in Revelation 14. **And she brought forth a man child, who was to rule all nations with a rod of iron: and her child was caught up unto God, and to his throne. And the woman fled into the wilderness** (Revelation 12:5,6). Out of the millions of Jews who have come from the twelve tribes of Israel, 144,000 will be caught up to God in the middle of the Tribulation Period. Why? **These were redeemed from among men, being the firstfruits unto God and to the Lamb** (Revelation 14:4). Those 144,000 will find favor with God and be caught up while the remaining millions of Jews will be left behind in the Tribulation Period.

Also note that the 144,000 are all men: **These are they which were not defiled with women; for they are virgins** (Revelation 14:4). **And in their mouth was found no guile: for they are without fault before the throne of God** (Revelation 14:5). Although the main part of the nation of Israel will not be caught up, that does not mean they will be lost. They will be saved, but they will be left behind to go through the whole Tribulation Period. It will be the same with the Gentile nations—when Jesus comes for the Gentile Bride, all of the Gentile Christians will not be caught up. Most of them will go into the Tribulation Period.

REASON FIFTEEN:
JUST A FEW WHO ARE ALIVE WILL BE CAUGHT UP.

For many are called, but few are chosen (Matthew 22:14). In Enoch's day, multitudes of people dwelt on the face of the Earth; but just one man was caught up to be with the Lord. When God destroyed the cities of Sodom and Gomorrah, four people started out of the city; but only three, Lot and his two daughters, made it all the way out. Little things can keep you out of the Rapture. Lot's wife only looked back at the city, and she was turned into a pillar of salt. **But his wife looked back from behind him, and she became a pillar of salt** (Genesis 19:26). Do you think God will excuse you for your disobediences when He did not excuse Lot's wife?

Neighbor, obey the Lord as Peter and the other apostles did when they said, **We ought to obey God rather than men** (Acts 5:29). In Noah's day, only eight people out of the multitudes who were on the face of the Earth went into the ark. The others were left outside to suffer the wrath of God. Those who have not received the Holy Ghost baptism when Jesus comes will also remain on Earth to suffer the wrath of God.

REASON SIXTEEN:
YOU MUST HAVE ON THE WHOLE ARMOR OF GOD.

Finally, my brethren, be strong in the Lord, and in the power of his might. Put on the whole armour of God, that ye may be able to stand against the wiles of the devil (Ephesians 6:10,11). You cannot be ready for the Rapture without the whole armor of God, and you cannot have that whole armor of God without having the Holy Ghost. Only yielding completely to Him gives you the armor of God.

Ephesians goes on to say, **Praying always with all prayer and supplication in the Spirit** (Ephesians 6:18). How can you pray in the Holy Spirit when you do not have Him? Paul said, **I will pray with the spirit** (I Corinthians 14:15).

REASON SEVENTEEN:
CHRIST IS OUR EXAMPLE.

For even hereunto were ye called: because Christ also suffered for us, leaving us an example, that ye should follow his steps (I Peter 2:21). Every miracle that Christ performed was through the Holy Ghost. Christ had the Holy Ghost when He ascended back to Heaven, so you must have Him to be caught up when Jesus comes. **But if the Spirit of him that raised up Jesus from the dead dwell in you, he that raised up Christ from the dead shall also quicken your mortal bodies by his Spirit that dwelleth in you** (Romans 8:11). It was the Holy Ghost who raised Jesus from the dead, and you must have the Holy Ghost *in* you to quicken your mortal body, too.

REASON EIGHTEEN:
RECEIVING THE HOLY GHOST IS A COMMANDMENT OF CHRIST.

And, being assembled together with them, [Jesus] **commanded them that they should not depart from Jerusalem, but wait for the promise of the Father, which, saith he, ye have heard of me. For John truly baptized**

with water; but ye shall be baptized with the Holy Ghost not many days hence (Acts 1:4,5). If the disciples had been to the Upper Room before that awful night in the Garden of Gethsemane, Peter would not have cut off a man's ear with a sword because he would have listened to the love teachings of Jesus who said, **If ye love me, keep my commandments** (John 14:15). In another place, the Bible says, **For this is the love of God, that we keep his commandments** (I John 5:3). If you don't love God enough to keep His commandments, you surely could not love Him enough to be raptured. You must follow the Lord all the way, and He commanded you to receive the Holy Ghost.

REASON NINETEEN:
A HUNGER FOR GOD IS A PART OF BEING READY FOR THE RAPTURE.

Blessed are they which do hunger and thirst after righteousness: for they shall be filled (Matthew 5:6). You have to have an appetite for and want the things of God; and if you hunger for God, He will give you the Holy Ghost. Then you have to hunger and thirst after righteousness so the Spirit can keep you filled.

If a son shall ask bread of any of you that is a father, will he give him a stone? or if he ask a fish, will he for a fish give him a serpent? Or if he shall ask an egg, will he offer him a scorpion? If ye then, being evil, know how to give good gifts unto your children: how much more shall your heavenly Father give the Holy Spirit to them that ask him (Luke 11:11–13)? A hunger for God will compel you to seek Him in His fullness, and the baptism of the Holy Ghost is part of that fullness. The Bible states, **Ask, and it shall be given you** (Matthew 7:7). God will give the Holy Spirit to those who ask.

REASON TWENTY:

SPEAK THE HEAVENLY LANGUAGE OF THE HOLY GHOST.

And when the king came in to see the guests, he saw there a man which had not on a wedding garment [the Holy Ghost]**: And he saith unto him, Friend** [Jesus called him a friend, not an enemy.], **how camest thou in hither not having a wedding garment**

[Without the wedding garment, he was not worthy to be part of the bridal party.]**? And he was speechless** (Matthew 22:11,12). That man did not have the Holy Ghost; therefore, he did not speak the heavenly language. To be changed and caught up when Jesus comes, you must have on the proper wedding garment and speak the heavenly language; and you cannot do those things unless you have the Holy Ghost.

Then said the king to the servants, Bind him hand and foot, and take him away, and cast him into outer darkness; there shall be weeping and gnashing of teeth (Matthew 22:13). In other words, without the garment of the Holy Ghost who gives the heavenly language, he was spewed into the Tribulation Period.

REASON TWENTY-ONE:
LAY ASIDE ALL THE WEIGHTS AND RECEIVE THE HOLY GHOST.

Wherefore seeing we also are compassed about with so great a cloud of witnesses, let us lay aside every weight, and the sin which doth so easily beset us, and let us run

with patience the race that is set before us, Looking unto Jesus the author and finisher of our faith (Hebrews 12:1,2). If you will lay aside all the weights and look to Jesus, He will give you the Holy Ghost. He said, **And I will pray the Father, and he shall give you another Comforter, that he may abide with you forever** (John 14:16).

You must look to Jesus with patience and continue to look. **Be ye also patient; stablish your hearts: for the coming of the Lord draweth nigh** (James 5:8). When you look at Jesus and keep your eyes on Him, you will keep your eyes on the Will, the Word, because the Spirit will remind you of it daily. The Will includes all the promises you need and lays out all the paths you must follow from here to Heaven. Receive the Holy Ghost.

REASON TWENTY-TWO:

THE HOLY GHOST WILL GIVE YOU FAITH TO MAKE THE RAPTURE.

Contend for the faith which was once delivered unto the saints (Jude 1:3). The faith that was delivered to the Early Church brought them to the place where they were baptized in the Holy Ghost. If we don't need such faith, why are we told to contend for it? We cannot have the fullness of God's faith without having the Holy Ghost dwelling within.

REASON TWENTY-THREE:
YOU MUST HAVE THE FRUITS OF THE SPIRIT THAT COME THROUGH THE HOLY GHOST.

But the fruit of the Spirit is love, joy, peace, longsuffering, gentleness, goodness, faith, Meekness, temperance (Galatians 5:22,23). To have the fullness of the nine fruits of the Spirit, you must have the Holy Ghost. There would be no apples without apple trees or pears without pear trees; and so there are no fruits of the Spirit in your life unless you receive the bearer of those fruits, the Holy Spirit.

REASON TWENTY-FOUR:
THE BRIDE WILL ACCEPT THE GIFTS OF THE SPIRIT.

How can the Bride accept the gifts of the Spirit when she rejects the Holy Ghost who is the giver of the gifts? Remember from Chapter One that Rebekah (a type of the Bride) accepted the gifts that Abraham's servant (a type of the Holy Ghost) offered her. Do you think she would have been accepted as the bride for Isaac had she refused the servant of Abraham and his gifts? Absolutely not. Neither will you be accepted as part of the Bride of Christ if you refuse to accept the Holy Ghost and His gifts.

REASON TWENTY-FIVE:
YOU WILL NOT ESCAPE IF YOU NEGLECT THE HOLY GHOST.

Therefore we ought to give the more earnest heed to the things which we have heard, lest at any time we should let them slip. For if the word spoken by angels was stedfast, and every transgression and disobedience received a just recompence of reward; How shall we escape, if we neglect so great salvation; which at the first began to be spoken by the Lord, and was confirmed unto us by them that heard him; God also bearing them witness, both with signs and wonders, and with divers miracles, and gifts of the Holy Ghost, according to his own will (Hebrews 2:1–4)? Paul was writing to Christians who already had salvation, so this great salvation he was telling them about was the Holy Ghost. How shall we escape the Tribulation Period if we neglect so great salvation?

REASON TWENTY-SIX:
YOU MUST HAVE THE SEAL OF GOD.

In whom ye also trusted, after that ye heard the word of truth, the gospel of your salvation: in whom also after that ye believed, ye were sealed with that holy Spirit of promise (Ephesians 1:13). Note that it says *after you heard the word of truth.* That means you were not sealed with the Holy Spirit until after you had believed and were saved. This seal only comes after your conversion just as Peter said, **Repent, and be baptized every one of you in the name of Jesus Christ for the remission of sins, and ye shall receive the gift of the Holy Ghost** (Acts 2:38). You must have the seal of God, which is the Holy Ghost, if you expect to be taken in the Rapture.

REASON TWENTY-SEVEN:
YOU WILL BE A WITNESS TO GOD'S POWER THROUGH THE HOLY GHOST.

Jesus told the disciples that after they had received the Holy Ghost, they would **be witnesses unto me both in Jerusalem, and in all Judaea, and in Samaria, and unto the uttermost part of the earth** (Acts 1:8). The Holy Spirit also testifies, and He is ready to use you to testify and to make you a witness; but you cannot be a real witness to the greatness of God's power without the Spirit's baptism. It takes the Holy Spirit to really make us witnesses, and He will draw people to us. Every Spirit-filled person is obligated to be His witness just as we are obligated to live pure, clean, holy and righteous just like Jesus did.

It takes great love to be a witness for the Lord, and it takes the Holy Ghost to give us that kind of love. **The love of God is shed abroad in our hearts by the Holy Ghost which is given unto us** (Romans 5:5), and that means that He also sheds abroad or flows that love into your mind.

Not only will the Holy Ghost help you prepare for the catching-away hour, He will help you give love to others and witness to them so they, too, can receive God's fullness. All that Christ brought—the freedom, the liberty and all the greatness of His love and faith—has to be poured to us through the invisible person, the Holy Ghost.

REASON TWENTY-EIGHT:
YOU CANNOT WITHSTAND GOD AND MAKE THE RAPTURE.

Forasmuch then as God gave them the like gift as he did unto us, who believed on the Lord Jesus Christ; what was I, that I could withstand God (Acts 11:17)? If you reject the Holy Ghost baptism, you are withstanding God. The Bible plainly states, **Forbid not to speak with tongues** (I Corinthians 14:39). To forbid tongues is withstanding God and failing to be at the place where the Holy Ghost can change you in a twinkling of an eye at the second coming of the Lord.

REASON TWENTY-NINE:
YOU MUST BE FOUND BLAMELESS THROUGH THE HOLY GHOST.

Wherefore, beloved, seeing that ye look for such things, be diligent that ye may be found of him in peace, without spot, and blameless (II Peter 3:14). **And unto them that look for him shall he appear the second time without sin unto salvation** (Hebrews 9:28). How can you truly be looking for Jesus to come unless you are blameless before Him? **Till we all come in the unity of the faith, and of the knowledge of the Son of God, unto a perfect man, unto the measure of the stature of the fulness of Christ** (Ephesians 4:13). You cannot have the fullness of Christ without first being blameless and then receiving the Holy Ghost. To be blameless, you must walk in the light; but if you don't, you will not be blameless in the eyes of the Lord. **But if we walk in the light, as he is in the light, we have fellowship one with another, and the blood of Jesus Christ his Son cleanseth us from all sin** (I John 1:7). You will be blameless when you have done all the Lord requires, and that includes receiving the Holy Ghost baptism. **Therefore to him that knoweth to do good, and doeth it not, to him it is sin** (James 4:17).

REASON THIRTY:
YIELD TO THE HOLY GHOST OR YOU WILL QUENCH THE SPIRIT.

The Holy Ghost is here on a mission to get the Bride ready for the coming of Christ, so how can anyone who quenches the Holy Ghost be ready for the Rapture? **Quench not the Spirit** (I Thessalonians 5:19). "Quench" means "to subdue, suppress, extinguish or make an end to." Do not smother the Spirit and let your spirit take over. Some of you have allowed unbelieving preachers and teachers to cause you to quench the Spirit, but no one who turns his back on the Holy Ghost baptism can be ready for the coming of the Lord. The Bible says we are to **rejoice evermore. Pray without ceasing. In every thing give thanks: for this is the will of God in Christ Jesus concerning you. Quench not the Spirit. Despise not prophesyings. Prove all things; hold fast that which is good. Abstain from**

all appearance of evil. And the very God of peace sanctify you wholly; and I pray God your whole spirit and soul and body be preserved blameless unto the coming of our Lord Jesus Christ (I Thessalonians 5:16–23). A person who does these things will receive the Holy Ghost; but if you quench the Spirit, there will not be enough of His power working in you to change you when Jesus comes.

GOD SPOKE TO ME

God has told me three times that the people who are alive when Jesus comes will need the Holy Ghost baptism, with the initial evidence of speaking with other tongues, to be changed on Rapture Day. God has given me numerous scriptures to back up what He said, and I have given them to you. The Lord also gave me special power to lay hands on people to receive the Holy Ghost just as the disciples did in the Early Church (Acts 8:17 and Acts 19:6). God told me to preach the Holy Ghost to the people, and Jesus is soon coming! Don't let anyone convince you that you do not need this glorious baptism because without it, you will go into the Tribulation

Period. After Jesus comes, it will be too late to change your mind and escape that devastating period. Humbly, I have given you these reasons as the Lord gave them to me. Now, I can say with Paul, **Wherefore I take you to record this day, that I am pure from the blood of all men. For I have not shunned to declare unto you all the counsel of God** (Acts 20:26,27).

CHAPTER 4

The Tongue and the Holy Ghost

In His great wisdom, God chose speaking in tongues as the initial evidence of the baptism of the Holy Spirit; but for some people, tongues is a great roadblock that the devil uses to keep them from believing in the person of the Holy Spirit and from receiving His wonderful baptism. The devil makes them afraid of tongues, and they back away.

Many people have disputed speaking in tongues, and many preachers have sent their own souls to hell by preaching against it. There will be more people in hell because of their tongues than for any other reason because the devil has made the tongue to be a curse when God created it to be one of man's greatest blessings. He was to have used it to talk to his God, but man sold out to the devil and lost that privilege.

I know of a minister who declared from the pulpit that speaking in other tongues came from hell and that it was going back there; and when he said that, the Spirit of God lifted from him. That man and his church members believed in regeneration and sanctification but not in the Holy Ghost baptism with the initial evidence of speaking in other tongues.

Later, that minister moved away to pastor another church, but God had never dealt with him again since he had made that statement. Then one day, while he was praying and seeking God, the Lord spoke to him and said, "You will have to go back and make what you said right or I will never forgive you."

You cannot talk against the Holy Ghost. When people associate this power with the devil, they are calling the Holy Ghost a devil. Some people even claim it is witchcraft, but that is blaspheming against the Holy Ghost;

and He will never again deal with people who say such things.

The Lord said, **Wherefore I say unto you, All manner of sin and blasphemy shall be forgiven unto men: but the blasphemy against the Holy Ghost shall not be forgiven unto men. And whosoever speaketh a word against the Son of man, it shall be forgiven him: but whosoever speaketh against the Holy Ghost, it shall not be forgiven him, neither in this world, neither in the world to come** (Matthew 12:31,32).

We are living in the most blasphemous hour that has ever been; it is even worse than it was in the days of Noah and Sodom and Gomorrah. It was terrible then; but now, all the puke of the devil is being spewed out for the final time. Many people will not listen to the tongue of the Spirit, and they have turned their backs on the prophecies of the Spirit and the messages in tongues and interpretations.

Thank God that the greatness and the power of God are falling like never before. The Bible said that the time would come when **whosoever shall call on the name of the**

Lord shall be saved (Acts 2:21). That hour is now, and whosoever calleth can come. We give people the Gospel; and they are delivered from witchcraft, voodooism and many other works of the devil in a matter of moments. They call unto the Lord, and He answers; and as they look to Him, He delivers them and sets them free.

THE TONGUE CAN BE A BLESSING OR A CURSE

The tongue is a valuable indication of the quality of a person's religion, so what quality is your religion? The Lord was so delighted and proud when He made man in the Garden of Eden and gave him a tongue and speech. Any of you parents can identify with how great it was when you heard your children speak their first words; but when God made Adam and Eve, they immediately had the gift of pure, wonderful speech and were able to talk to God. He was the one who gave human beings their speech, and He places great honor on it.

God made man, but many people are so ignorant that they deny it. Some will even say there is no God, but the Bible says they are just fools. **The fool hath said in his heart, There is no God** (Psalm 14:1). How pitiful it will be when people find out too late that God is real after all and that He did make man.

The power and influence that the right kind of speech can have for God are wonderful. Divine love, hope and grace go forth in the right kind of speech; but James says the tongue can also be a mighty power of evil influence. **The tongue is a fire, a world of iniquity: so is the tongue among our members, that it defileth the whole body, and setteth on fire the course of nature; and it is set on fire of hell** (James 3:6).

See how damnable the tongue can be? It can defile the whole body; but when it is used as God willed it to be used, it can edify the body. When God created man, He made the beautiful tongue to be the greatest faculty of the flesh. Consider what power the tongue and speech can have, what they can do for people and how they can help and deliver them. God can use the tongue more than the eyes, the ears or even the hands; and the Lord wants you to know that.

The Lord chose the tongue and the control of it through the means of true salvation to manifest the mastery over man's entire nature. Some people think they can never master self or their emotions, but the Bible says they can. **For in many things we offend all. If any man offend not in word, the same is a perfect man, and able also to bridle the whole body** (James 3:2). When you can control your tongue, you can control your whole body; but when you fail to control your tongue, you will not have control over the rest of your body like you should.

If you do not wear the love bridle, the Bible says you have no salvation; and many people are deceived because they do not wear that love bridle. **If any man among you seem to be religious, and bridleth not his tongue, but deceiveth his own heart, this man's religion is vain** (James 1:26). It is dangerous to use your tongue in the wrong way in this hour. If you fail to wear the love bridle, you will grieve the Holy Spirit; and He cannot make Himself real to you.

WHAT KIND OF TONGUE DO YOU HAVE?

For every kind of beasts, and of birds, and of serpents, and of things in the sea, is tamed, and hath been tamed of mankind: But the tongue can no man tame; it is an unruly evil, full of deadly poison (James 3:7,8). Is your tongue unruly? If you are not consecrated to God and wearing the love bridle, it is; and you may think you will get into Heaven like that, but you won't. It is dangerous for the tongue not to have a sanctified, consecrated heart behind it because then it is full of deadly poison. Nevertheless, people like that will still claim to be all right and on their way to Heaven. When you have a tongue of the blood of Jesus Christ, there is no poison in it.

The Lord made man with a holy tongue; and he was never to speak one word of evil or hate, not one false statement or anything unclean. The tongue in Eden was as holy as God's tongue, and it used the same speech that God spoke. It is no wonder God chose tongues as the first evidence of the baptism of the Holy Ghost, but the Lord lost man completely when He lost man's tongue. You cannot keep control over your tongue within yourself. It moves too fast even for you, so you have to have the presence of the person of the Holy Ghost to help you. However, if God has lost your tongue, you are not one of His no matter how much you think you are.

There are people who always mind the business of others, and some say that it is because they have no business of their own. People who have plenty of their own things to do are busy taking care of them. The Lord teaches us not to be busybodies because when you are, your tongue is greatly involved—it is leading you right on. Paul said to one church, **For we hear that there are some which walk among you disorderly, working not at all, but are busybodies. Now them that are such we command and exhort by our Lord Jesus Christ, that with quietness they work, and eat their own bread** (II Thessalonians 3:11,12).

GOSSIP IS DANGEROUS

Jesus and the Holy Spirit are so grieved and insulted when you gossip instead of ministering the Word to people. You should tell others what God has said instead of what people have said. Some people have a long tongue, a dirty mouth and a filthy soul; yet you pass on what they tell you.

Why don't you put on the love bridle so the Holy Spirit can use the whole you? If you are not perfect in speech, He cannot use you in perfection. You cannot say things that hurt people and then expect to be used by the Holy Spirit because He will not use you. You are deceiving your own heart if you think He will.

The tongue is such a measuring rod with God that we have to take heed and check our tongues every day to make sure we have not said anything that the Lord would not have said, and we must never even want to say such things. If you do not know what to say, just ask yourself, "What would Jesus say? What would Jesus talk about?" You can go to the Bible, the record of His life on Earth, and find out what He had to say. The things He said were always profitable and edifying, and they lifted people up.

Some people's tongues have caused them

so much trouble because they gossip. They don't call it gossip, yet they talk when they have no business talking. They cause trouble and even try to match couples together, and that is dangerous. Stay out of people's lives; let the Holy Spirit take care of them. If you give advice to someone, you had better make sure it is the will of God because the Lord will hold you responsible for it.

I fear God, and I depend on Him for answers. When I give advice, I want to know it is God's advice, that it is what He wants the person to hear. Some of you blurt out things you should never say and tell people things you should just keep out of. Then the Spirit cannot use you because you are out of God's will. You may need some special wisdom and knowledge from God; but you are out of place, so you miss it. Then you wonder, "Why did that happen? Why did I make that mistake? Why didn't I make the right decision?" It was because you were out of place and doing something that the Lord did not will for you to do.

The tongue possesses great power for good

when it is given to God. It is a great power for God and a great power in your life when you use your tongue to speak to the Lord, to rebuke the devil, to talk faith and to encourage yourself and others, especially children of God. Even a sinner can speak good words, and some speak more good than others; but when you come to God, you are to speak all good. What kind of tongue do you have? Tell me the kind of tongue you have, and I will tell you what kind of religion you have.

USE YOUR TONGUE FOR GOD

The Holy Ghost baptism is a gift of grace; and when you are baptized in the Holy Ghost, it signifies that you have all the divine favor of God. At last, God has you completely; and the Holy Spirit has you completely when He gets your tongue. The Bible tells us, **For with the heart man believeth unto righteousness; and with the mouth confession is made unto salvation** (Romans 10:10). You must use your tongue to confess your sins to God in the first place, and then the salvation of the world is dependent upon the tongue as we take Jesus to the world.

Then Paul said, **Unto me, who am less than the least of all saints, is this grace given, that I should preach among the Gentiles the unsearchable riches of Christ** (Ephesians 3:8). The tongue is so important that it is used to declare the unsearchable riches of Christ. Our human tongues must be used to get this Gospel to the whole world, to help pull down Heaven and the power of God, to help send rockets of power to the inhabitants of the Earth and to shake people up with earthquakes of power.

You can use your tongue to talk to God at any time, and He hears a holy tongue just like He heard Adam and Eve in Eden. With delight, He hears every word you say and rejoices because the human race can have holy speech once again.

How fitting it is that speech has been singled out as the most important of all our faculties. Do you now see how God can use the tongue and why He puts such honor on speech? Do you see why He has been so careful to give you salvation and the love bridle so you can have a holy tongue? If the Israelites had possessed this holy tongue on their journey, they would have gone straight into Canaan. The Lord would have driven out the seven nations that were there, and how heavenly it would have been...but their tongues got them into trouble.

THE SPIRIT MUST USE YOUR TONGUE

The devil tells some of you who are seeking the Holy Ghost baptism that you are not worthy; and, of course, no one is worthy of the Holy Ghost. You were not worthy of salvation either, but the Lord counted you worthy because He looked at you through the blood. When you accept that divine blood, it makes you worthy in the eyes of God; and when the tongue is sanctified and made holy through the blood of the Lamb, then the temple, the body, is ready for the Holy Ghost to move into. When He baptizes you, He actually takes control of your unworthy tongue; and your tongue becomes His.

The Holy Spirit cannot baptize you until He can baptize the whole you, and He has to have the tongue first of all. The tongue has to be 100 percent pure and as holy as Heaven itself before the Holy Ghost can use it, and it must remain clean for Him to continue to use it. You may get your tongue all cleaned up, and the Holy Ghost may come in; but you must keep your tongue clean. The Bible says, **Let all bitterness, and wrath, and anger, and clamour, and evil speaking, be put away from you, with all malice: And be ye kind one to another, tenderhearted, forgiving one another, even as God for Christ's sake hath forgiven you** (Ephesians 4:31,32).

When the Holy Ghost speaks, it is 100 percent divinity speaking. That is why we are not to teach people to talk in tongues, and there is no such thing with God as speaking in tongues at will. The devil brought that into the Church of Jesus Christ to destroy the real baptism of the Spirit and the real power of God. You must have a real tongue of the Spirit and the true reality of the baptism, and this should not scare you if you know you have the real thing.

If you can speak in tongues any time you get ready, that is not the holy tongue of the Spirit. To receive the real baptism of the Holy Ghost is to be baptized with the Spirit just as the disciples were on the Day of Pentecost. The

Holy Spirit gave them the utterance, and that is the way it always must be. **And they were all filled with the Holy Ghost, and began to speak with other tongues, as the Spirit gave them utterance** (Acts 2:4).

The disciples furnished their tongues, and the Holy Spirit took complete control of their tongues and spoke any language through them that He wanted to. They spoke in over fourteen different languages, and the people from different nations and places who had gathered there were amazed. **And they were all amazed and marvelled, saying one to another, Behold, are not all these which speak Galilaeans? And how hear we every man in our own tongue, wherein we were born? Parthians, and Medes, and Elamites, and the dwellers in Mesopotamia, and in Judaea, and Cappadocia, in Pontus, and Asia, Phrygia, and Pamphylia, in Egypt, and in the parts of Libya about Cyrene, and strangers of Rome, Jews and proselytes, Cretes and Arabians, we do hear them speak in our tongues the wonderful works of God** (Acts 2:7–11).

The people knew they were hearing the wonderful works of God being spoken, and that was exactly what the baptism was, too; but they did not know the Holy Spirit, and many of them mocked His baptism. They thought the disciples were drunk; but Peter said, **For these are not drunken, as ye suppose, seeing it is but the third hour of the day. But this is that which was spoken by the prophet Joel** (Acts 2:15,16). Peter pointed the people to the scriptures, and they should have known them; but when you do not take time to read what God has said or given through His holy prophets, then you are in trouble.

Some people may take time to read the Bible, but they do not always take time to believe it. You have to stay with it and believe it. The Lord said in the last days He would pour His Spirit out upon all flesh, and that is what He is doing: **And it shall come to pass in the last days, saith God, I will pour out of my Spirit upon all flesh: and your sons and your daughters shall prophesy, and your young men shall see visions, and your old men shall dream dreams** (Acts 2:17).

PREPARE TO RECEIVE

The Holy Spirit had to get the disciples' minds ready before He could descend from Heaven on them; they did not just go to the Upper Room and suddenly there was a sound from Heaven. Even after all the Lord had taught them, it took them days to get ready; but it does not matter how many days it took because what counts is that they tarried until. Jesus had anointed them with praises and told them not to start the Church until they had received the Holy Ghost. **And, behold, I send the promise of my Father upon you: but tarry ye in the city of Jerusalem, until ye be endued with power from on high** (Luke 24:49).

The disciples were not in one mind and one accord at first, but they finally came into that oneness. **Then returned they unto Jerusalem from the mount called Olivet, which is from Jerusalem a sabbath day's journey. And when they were come in, they went up into an upper room, where abode both Peter, and James, and John, and Andrew, Philip, and Thomas, Bartholomew, and Matthew,**

James the son of Alphaeus, and Simon Zelotes, and Judas the brother of James. These all continued with one accord in prayer and supplication, with the women, and Mary the mother of Jesus, and with his brethren (Acts 1:12–14).

You have to prepare to receive the Holy Ghost and come into one mind with the truth. He is the Spirit of truth, and He will not come in if you are not in harmony with the truth. The devil offers counterfeits for everything God hands out, but the Spirit of truth will let you know what is real and what is not.

Receiving the Holy Ghost is not a time-consuming thing; it is a time of yielding to the Lord, and it is all about the way you yield. You have to be willing to do the whole will of God. You must also have your first love, a praise for God and gratitude for your salvation. You have to have a tongue of praise, and your whole being must be on fire with those praises. Then when the Spirit comes in, He will electrify you; and you will have a tongue of fire.

One day, everybody will speak the holy

speech of the Holy Spirit, the heavenly language. The Holy Spirit speaks that heavenly language now through those who have the Holy Ghost, and He speaks other languages as well. The holy, pure language that the Lord gave the first man and woman is no doubt the language that we will all speak in Heaven. We will speak it at will then because we will have glorified bodies and glorified speech; but until then, we do not have the power to speak Heaven's language at will—the Holy Ghost must speak it through us. The speaking with tongues is a symbol of the heavenly speech to come.

THE SPIRIT OF TRUTH

Critics can always find fault with the true baptism. They may think they are finding fault with Bible Pentecostal people, but they are really finding fault with God. We do not have an experience of our own; we have the Lord's experience. We do not have *our* Holy Ghost; we have *His* Holy Ghost, the tongue of *His* fire and the Spirit of truth.

The Holy Spirit is the source of truth, and He uses the tongue to speak only the truth through a person. When a person receives the Holy Spirit, the first thing the Holy Ghost usually does when He comes in is glorify Jesus. That is remarkable, but Jesus said it would be: **He** [the Holy Spirit] **shall glorify me** (John 16:14).

Jesus is our Lord, Master, Savior and coming King. He is **King of kings, and Lord of lords** (I Timothy 6:15), but He never glorified Himself when He was here—He glorified the Father. Neither will the Holy Ghost ever glorify Himself; He will glorify Jesus. You cannot glorify Jesus in your spirit without the truth because outside of truth there is no glory of God, and you cannot glorify the Lord Jesus unless you have divine glory to do it with.

For the Holy Spirit to live with you all the time, you have to be conscious of His presence. Then prayer and fasting will become different. When you pick up the Word—the truth—it will be different because you will know that the Spirit of truth is inside you fellowshipping with you; and He only fellowships through truth, never outside of it. He will walk hand-in-hand with you through truth, and He will lead you into the deepness of the love and peace of God.

There is nothing in the world like receiving the gift of the Holy Ghost. It is different from salvation, and it had to be. Some people claim that faith is the evidence of the Holy Ghost, and others claim that love is the evidence; but you receive all of those things in salvation. The Lord chose tongues as the evidence because it was a uniform evidence; and all people—the educated and the uneducated, the intelligent and the ignorant—could receive the same baptism and have the same sign.

It does not matter how many educational degrees people might have; when they get the Holy Ghost, He speaks a simple language. When people receive Jesus Christ in our overseas crusades, we take them right on through to the Holy Ghost baptism. Many of them cannot even read or write; but they still receive the same Holy Ghost, and a beautiful language comes forth.

Now, we do not all act the same way when we receive the Holy Ghost; there are different manifestations. Some people laugh, some shout and some praise God. There are so many different manifestations of the Spirit, and He deals with your personality. Some people are just more emotional than others.

MANIFESTATIONS OF THE SPIRIT

The Bible says, **Whosoever compoundeth** [maketh] **any like it** [the anointing oil], **or whosoever putteth any of it upon a stranger, shall even be cut off from his people** (Exodus 30:33). In Old Testament times, the anointing oil, a type of the Spirit, was not to be imitated; but today, people who talk in tongues at will are mimicking the Holy Spirit. They do not get ready to receive the real Spirit; so they try to make their tongue sound like the tongue of the Spirit, and that is as dangerous as eternal damnation itself. It is awful when people try to fool themselves into thinking that they have the Spirit of truth abiding within them when He is not there at all. It is a lie of the devil, and it is not the Spirit.

Some people think that any amount of earnestness or zeal can stand in the place of the Holy Spirit; and they think that emotionalism—swinging their hands and arms around and knocking into people—is the power of the Holy Ghost. Others will watch those with the Spirit and try to imitate them; but then they go beyond to put on a big show thinking, "If somebody can have the Holy Ghost because they move around a little, I can really show them how to move." The devil and people can imitate the real power of God, but they can never copy it.

All there is about some people is a shout. In some Pentecostal churches, the people gather together to whoop and holler and run in the aisles, and some even roll on the floor; but it is not for real. People like that may thunder; but God is not really blessing them, and they have no quickening or searching fire of the Holy Ghost. People must worship the Lord from the heart and really mean it. When people have the true tongue of fire, it is not in the thunder; it is in the lightning.

When lightning strikes the Earth, it causes fires; but thunder doesn't do that. Thunder may scare you, but it is not dangerous; however, lightning can kill you when it strikes. Thunder roars, and that is all many people do—they just shake you up with their big mouths and a lot of noise. They shout, "I have it!" Well, they have it all right, but I don't want any of it!

Always remember that when the thunder roars, you have to wait and see if there is any lightning to go with it, any fire of the Holy Ghost. If the tongue of fire is not there, the real Holy Ghost is not there. People cannot be baptized in the Holy Ghost today until they get the tongue of fire. When people imitate the Holy Spirit, it will show up on them sooner or later. **Wherefore by their fruits ye shall know them** (Matthew 7:20). If you do not have the right spirit, you will not have the right kind of fruit. What kind of spirit do you have?

We must have the real Holy Ghost with all the powers of Heaven. He helped God speak this universe into existence. He helped speak the stars, the moon and the sun into the skies. He helped make the green grass, the trees, the fishes, the waters and all life here on Earth. There is nothing but life in Him.

DO NOT BE DECEIVED

Some people hate the speaking with tongues, but how can you hate any part of God's Word? Remember again that when the disciples received the Holy Ghost on the Day of Pentecost, they **began to speak with other tongues, as the Spirit gave them utterance** (Acts 2:4). They did not speak in tongues until that time. Many who are deceived will say, "I have the Holy Ghost, but I do not speak with tongues." Then they do not have the Holy Ghost because when He comes in, He will speak. This is God's baptism from Heaven, so He has the right to say how it must be received and what the first thing will be that will happen when the Holy Ghost comes in.

Some people who claim to be Christians and yet object to the speaking in tongues say you cannot limit God to only one way of getting the Holy Ghost, but the Lord limited Himself to only one thing that could make atonement for the soul—the blood. He limited Himself to only one name through which to receive salvation—the name of Jesus. **Neither is there salvation in any other: for there**

is none other name under heaven given among men, whereby we must be saved (Acts 4:12).

God has the power to limit Himself or not to limit Himself. He has all power to do anything in any way He wants to, but people do not realize it. He gave us water baptism as the symbol of the death and resurrection of Christ, only one symbol and only one way. **Therefore we are buried with him by baptism into death: that like as Christ was raised up from the dead by the glory of the Father, even so we also should walk in newness of life** (Romans 6:4). At the Lord's Supper, He gave us Holy Communion in remembrance of Him. **And he took bread, and gave thanks, and brake it, and gave unto them, saying, This is my body which is given for you: this do in remembrance of me** (Luke 22:19).

Many people want to know why I stress tongues rather than the mighty wind or the fiery tongues that appeared on the Day of Pentecost. It is because those things were just symbols of the Holy Ghost. When He moved in that day, the person of the Holy Spirit filled the disciples' tabernacles of clay with more light, more glory and more of the reality of the presence of God than they had ever had. He filled them with more of the will of I-Am and with more of the peace, goodness and gentleness of I-Am.

If there is any deceit in you today, let the Holy Spirit use the blood and take it all away so you can see yourself as God sees you and not as you want to believe yourself to be. **For if any be a hearer of the word, and not a doer, he is like unto a man beholding his natural face in a glass: For he beholdeth himself, and goeth his way, and straightway forgetteth what manner of man he was. But whoso looketh into the perfect law of liberty, and continueth therein, he being not a forgetful hearer, but a doer of the work, this man shall be blessed in his deed** (James 1:23–25).

The Holy Spirit will lift you up before the mirror of God's Word; and if you will yield to the way you really look, you will cry out for mercy. He will change you through the blood, and all that is unlike the Lord will flow out of you so you can be the person the Lord desires you to be. You will have no trouble fitting your hands into His, and you will have no trouble making steps that are the same as His.

TAKE THE THOUGHTS OF GOD

The Bible says, **The Spirit searcheth all things, yea, the deep things of God** (I Corinthians 2:10). Notice that He searcheth *all* things. He searches us, and He searches out the deep thoughts of God to serve to us daily if we will receive them.

The Bible tells us to have the thoughts of God and to think deep, but many people are not aware of it. **O LORD, how great are thy works! and thy thoughts are very deep** (Psalm 92:5). The Holy Spirit gives me so many deep thoughts that are beyond me, thoughts I never received from any teacher at theological school or public school. The Holy Spirit's thoughts bless me, and He will serve you wonderful, deep thoughts, too. Some of you think you cannot have the right thought life, but that is because you will not let the Holy Spirit serve you.

The Spirit searches out everything for you, and He knows all about you. He knows why you are who you are and why your personality is like it is. If your personality needs to be changed, just yield to the Spirit; and He will change it. When He comes in and takes over, He blends your personality daily with the personality of Jesus Christ.

All of this is about the Holy Spirit working for us; and if we would only realize that He is working on our behalf, we would have it made. If we would come into the reality of this, we would not walk in fear, depression or despair like some people do. The disciples had to come into this reality, but Jesus had a hard time bringing them into it. He told them, **And when they bring you unto the synagogues, and unto magistrates, and powers, take ye no thought how or what thing ye shall answer, or what ye shall say: For the Holy Ghost shall teach you in the same hour what ye ought to say** (Luke 12:11,12). When you are brought before your persecutors, take no thought of what you are going to say; the Holy Ghost will give it to you. The

Holy Ghost will give you other things that you need in the same way if you are on the receiving side of the table; but you have to stay on the receiving side, the humility side and the side for people who wear the love bridle.

If you do not wear the love bridle, the receiving side of God's table is not for you; but with the love bridle on, the Holy Spirit is always there to serve you. Then He will give you what you need to say.

LET THE HOLY SPIRIT WORK IN YOUR MIND

The Holy Spirit will also give you the thoughts you need to dwell on; but if you let the devil crowd in to feed you other thoughts, then you back the Spirit away by yielding to that other spirit. It is so easy to yield to the spirit of the devil through your feelings because he works through feelings. He also works through your nervous system, but the Lord works through faith.

In Philippians, the Lord told us six things to think on. **Finally, brethren, whatsoever things are true, whatsoever things are honest, whatsoever things are just, whatsoever things are pure, whatsoever**

things are lovely, whatsoever things are of good report; if there be any virtue, and if there be any praise, think on these things (Philippians 4:8). Have you learned those six things? How can the Holy Ghost use them in your life if you don't know what they are? The Holy Spirit wants to feed you all of those lovely thoughts because they come from truth, the Word.

God has given you your thought life in the Holy Scriptures if you will only realize it. Divine love, peace, joy and contentment are there; and so are the plain paths for your feet. You will find everything you need to think on in the Word of God. The Bible tells us, **Trust in the LORD with all thine heart; and lean not unto thine own understanding. In all thy ways acknowledge him, and he shall direct thy paths** (Proverbs 3:5,6). The Lord promised to direct all of your paths when they are the paths of His divine will. The Lord is seeking to make Himself so real to you. Acknowledge Him in all of your thoughts.

The devil will bring you bad thoughts, but you do not have to keep them. Somebody may knock on your door and have a package for you, but you can accept it or reject it. So it is with the devil—when he knocks on your door with his thoughts, you can accept them or reject them. What will you do? I say, "Beat it, Devil!"

Give the Spirit first place to work with you and to help you each day. When you wake up, let Him have the privilege of giving you the first thoughts of the day; but know that the enemy will be right there to give you his thoughts, too. The old self will also try to give you thoughts if you do not have him buried deep enough.

The new self is the one who can associate with the person of the Holy Spirit. That self has a sanctified mind, and the Holy Spirit can give him thoughts just like He gave them to Jesus when He was on Earth.

JESUS, OUR EXAMPLE

When Jesus came, He came as a man. He **took upon him the form of a servant, and was made in the likeness of men** (Philippians 2:7). That was why it was necessary for Him to be baptized in water and to receive the gift of the Holy Ghost. Then after Jesus had received the Holy Ghost, the Spirit had to work through Him just like He was going to work through Peter, James and John. All of the gentleness, kindness and greatness that Jesus showed in His ministry flowed through Him as a man by the power of the Holy Ghost. It was all being demonstrated right before the disciples' eyes. They were receiving teaching from every move Jesus made, whether they knew it or not. He taught them how He depended on the Father to give Him what to say; and He told them, **For I have not spoken of myself; but the Father which sent me, he gave me a commandment, what I should say, and what I should speak. And I know that his commandment is life everlasting: whatsoever I speak therefore, even as the Father said unto me, so I speak** (John 12:49,50).

The Son could hear what the Father was saying, and we must say the things the Holy Ghost gives us to say, too; He gets those things from the Lord in Heaven. He speaks everything the Father wants the Bride to know, and the Bride must have ears to hear

Him. I say again that the Holy Ghost has come to serve you so you can serve others; then He will serve you things for your mind and help you, too, if you let Him.

Some of you allow your mind to get in such an awful shape at times. The devil comes against you, and it seems like all hell is boiling over on you. You are going through so much that it seems like a hammer is beating in your head, and you cannot stop it; but the Holy Spirit can stop it. He will use the blood on your mind, and He will take those thoughts if you will willingly give them to Him...but you have to give them to Him.

The Bible says, **Cast thy burden upon the LORD, and he shall sustain thee: he shall never suffer the righteous to be moved** (Psalm 55:22). You have to give your thoughts over to the Holy Spirit and then take your mind at once to the thought of a lost world. When you do that, the Spirit will give you other beautiful thoughts to go with it and let you know how precious you are in the eyes of God in this final hour. He will let you know that you are chosen by the Lord to get this

Gospel to the world and that the Lord loves you for letting the fruits of the Spirit be produced in your life.

The Spirit will deal with you about the soon coming of the Lord and how wonderful the Rapture is going to be. He will let you know the value of leading just one soul to the Lord and that all Heaven rejoices over that soul. Jesus said, **Joy shall be in heaven over one sinner that repenteth, more than over ninety and nine just persons, which need no repentance** (Luke 15:7). What beautiful thoughts those are. It makes me weep to think that the Spirit is so lowly and humble for us.

A LIFE OF BEAUTY

God Almighty planned all of this for us; and, oh, how He loves humanity! He created man and woman to have always been with Him in beauty, love, holiness and righteousness. The Bible tells us, **For the LORD taketh pleasure in his people: he will beautify the meek with salvation** (Psalm 149:4). Sin made man ugly, but no longer do we have to be ugly in the Lord's sight. He does not look at our skin that is wrinkling and getting old because the part that will live with Him forever will be without wrinkle, blemish or spot. What beauty that is before the Lord!

We are more beautiful to God than Lucifer ever was, and he was the most beautiful angel God had ever made; but your beauty has come through the Sacrificial Lamb, the Son of God. The Holy Spirit is like a beautician; and He can perform any kind of spiritual service needed to help you look, walk and talk exactly like the Lord wants us to.

The Lord is changing the children of God, and He has already changed us in many ways so that love and faith can flow from us. Our self-control flows out to people, and many of them are not used to seeing personalities that are so calm in times of trouble and storm. That is the Jesus way, and we are walking in His steps and sitting where He sat again and again.

The children of God have taken Jesus' place at the well, and the lost are coming to that well of salvation where we serve them the Gospel message. We have the personality of Jesus and wear the shoes of Jesus, so we talk like Him and act like Him. Just as the Holy

Spirit could take Jesus' tongue and speak at any time, the Holy Spirit can take our tongues and speak at any time through those of us who are really dedicated, consecrated, yielded and living pure, clean and holy before the Lord.

THE SPIRIT BRINGS THE REALITY OF THE WORD

When Jesus was here, He used personal pronouns when speaking of the Holy Ghost, which means that the Spirit is a person. **Howbeit when *he*, the Spirit of truth, is come, *he* will guide you into all truth: for *he* shall not speak of *himself*; but whatsoever *he* shall hear, that shall *he* speak: and *he* will shew you things to come. *He* shall glorify me: for *he* shall receive of mine, and shall shew it unto you. All things that the Father hath are mine: therefore said I, that *he* shall take of mine, and shall shew it unto you** (John 16:13–15).

It is marvelous indeed to have such a divine person living on the inside of us. He is not an energy, but He has plenty of spiritual energy to give to us; and you can have it because it is for all. He is not a presence but a real person who brings the presence of the Lord in like a mighty force, and He keeps that presence with you in the inner man. The Holy Ghost is not a power; but He brings power, gives power and uses power through us.

Be conscious of the person of the Holy Spirit when you pray, and your prayers will be exciting. He will lead you to the Word and be right there to teach you, and you will be amazed at the understanding He will give you. Never tell the Holy Spirit that you cannot learn. Instead, say, "Holy Spirit, I can do all things through the Word and through the Lord because you are with me." **I can do all things through Christ which strengtheneth me** (Philippians 4:13).

You have to give over to a teacher if you want to be taught; and you cannot learn it all in one day, one week, one month or even one year. The Spirit teaches you as one person teaches another, and then you will come into the light of the Word. **Study to shew thyself approved unto God, a workman that needeth not to be ashamed, rightly dividing the word of truth** (II Timothy 2:15).

The Holy Ghost is the author of the Holy Bible, and He is the one who can help you understand what God meant. God gave the Bible to the Holy Ghost so He could give it to mankind, but you have to listen.

I get so carried away with the Word that my time with the Lord just flies. The Lord lifts me into lofty heights through His mighty power, and He takes over my eyes and lets me see as He sees. He uses my mind to think His thoughts, and it is wonderful to be lifted above this sin-cursed world into such a heavenly place with Him. The Bible tells us all about it in the Word. **But God, who is rich in mercy, for his great love wherewith he loved us… hath raised us up together, and made us sit together in heavenly places in Christ Jesus** (Ephesians 2:4,6).

I have spent thousands and thousands of hours studying the Word, the Book of all books. Some of you think that you cannot understand it, and you can't just by reading it. You have to live it, and it has to become a part of you. Every word God speaks stands alone, and each one will continue to do so for all eternity. **But the word of the Lord endureth forever** (I Peter 1:25).

Some people do not really know the Word; they just think they do, and they do not even know the truth when they hear it or read it. I give people truth, and I give them the Word of God to back it up. That is why so many have accepted the truth, and their lives have been changed.

SEE CLEARLY THROUGH THE SPIRIT

Can you feel the quickening of the person of the Holy Ghost on the inside of you? The life of the blood flows greatly through Him. He has complete understanding of the blood and salvation, but we do not. We see through a glass darkly; but one day, we will see in all light just as Paul wrote to the Corinthians. **For now we see through a glass, darkly; but then face to face** (I Corinthians 13:12).

We cannot see everything, but the Holy Spirit can. He uses perfect faith to reveal the things of God to us, and He uses perfect love to bring us into that perfect faith. The Holy Spirit takes you by the hand and leads you to where you should go, and He will bring you into greater and greater things as He serves you with such gladness.

The Holy Spirit is so jubilant in the lives of the very consecrated and dedicated today, those who are really serving God and are not using their tongues in the wrong way, those who have no gossip, scorn, envy, strife, resentment or rebellion in them. The dedicated use no unclean or bad words, and they do not say things they shouldn't. The Holy Spirit uses our mouths, so they must be clean and righteous mouths.

Your tongue must be available to the Holy Spirit at any time. You gave it completely over to the Holy Spirit when He baptized you; and you signified that you did by saying, "You have the whole me." No matter how close a person has been to you, no one has ever had the whole you before. No one has been able to use your tongue to speak in any language he or she wanted to, but the person of the Holy Spirit can because He is really miraculous!

The Bible says, **Greater is he that is in you, than he that is in the world** (I John 4:4). This is talking about the Holy Ghost, and that says it all; so why should you be afraid of man or devil? We have the history of the martyrs who overcame in the Early Church because they had the Holy Spirit and because they knew and recognized Him.

The Holy Spirit was sent to get a Bride ready for Jesus, and He is working diligently to do that. We cannot afford to fail in this hour, and He who is within us will see that we don't as we yield completely to Him. Nothing will be able to stop us. When the Holy Spirit can bring you to the place where you give everything over to Him—even your life—and you have nothing more to give, then you are receiving. Keep what you have given to Him in His hands and never take those things away.

KEEP THE STORMS OUT

When you have the Holy Ghost inside, He will give you peace and joy and flow the love of God into your mind; but some of you have so much trouble within because you allow the storms to get inside.

One day, the disciples were on the stormy deep with Jesus; and they thought their boat was about to sink. **And there arose a great**

storm of wind, and the waves beat into the ship, so that it was now full. And he was in the hinder part of the ship, asleep on a pillow: and they awake him, and say unto him, Master, carest thou not that we perish? And he arose, and rebuked the wind, and said unto the sea, Peace, be still. And the wind ceased, and there was a great calm (Mark 4:37–39).

Jesus had no storm inside of Him on that boat; but the disciples had allowed the storm to get on the inside, and it was destroying them. They were so scared that they grabbed Jesus and shook Him, but Jesus had peace because He had the Comforter. He did not depend on man's hands to help Him; He was in the hands of the Father and the Holy Spirit, so He simply rose up and said, *Peace, be still.*

You have to keep the storms outside of you for the peace of God that passeth all understanding to reign on the inside. **And the peace of God, which passeth all understanding, shall keep your hearts and minds through Christ Jesus** (Philippians 4:7). The Holy Spirit produces the wonderful fruits of peace, joy, love and anything else you need; and you cannot find those things anywhere on Earth except through the Lord. **Now the God of hope fill you with all joy and peace in believing, that ye may abound in hope, through the power of the Holy Ghost** (Romans 15:13). That means you are to abound in everything that God has promised through the power of the Holy Ghost. What an Eden we can have on the inside of us with the Spirit as our caretaker.

The Rapture is just ahead; but I still see multitudes of people who need to be won, and we must be ready to serve them. We can only serve what we have, and we must receive so much from the Lord. We will not serve hate because we will have love. We will not serve strife because we will have peace. We will not serve a haughty spirit because we will have a humble spirit. The Bride will serve people just like Jesus did when He was here.

CHAPTER 5

The Person of the Holy Ghost

Jesus promised us abundant life. **I am come that they might have life, and that they might have it more abundantly** (John 10:10). However, you must have the Holy Spirit in your life to have that abundant life. You may enjoy some blessings without the baptism, but you will not have the abundant life that will allow the Holy Spirit to get things done.

It was actually greater for us for the Holy Spirit, the invisible person, to come than for Jesus to have stayed on Earth because, as a man, Jesus had limited Himself. However, the Holy

Spirit is wherever you are because He lives on the inside of you if you have His baptism.

God chose tongues as the initial evidence of the Holy Ghost because it reveals the personality of the Spirit; but even many people who have the Holy Spirit baptism do not know how real He is, so they will not let Him be as real as He wants to be. They do not realize that this invisible person actually moves in to dwell in our bodies, our temples of clay. **What? know ye not that your body is the temple of the Holy Ghost which is in you, which ye have of God, and ye are not your own** (I Corinthians 6:19)? If Jesus had not come, the Holy Ghost never would have come because He will only move into a temple that is divine blood clean. Jesus paid the price to make it possible for us to be blood pure and blood clean so the Holy Ghost could move in.

It is impossible to know the whole truth without the Holy Spirit baptism because the Spirit is the only one who can teach you all about Jesus. I can tell you what the Bible says about Jesus, about my experiences with Him and about His visitations with me; but

I cannot tell you all about Him. No human being knows all about Jesus, but the Holy Spirit does because He has known Jesus for trillions of years. He knows why He came; He knows every word He spoke while He was on Earth, and He even knows things that were not recorded in the Bible.

John said that if all the acts of Christ were recorded, there would not be enough places to put all the books they would fill. **And there are also many other things which Jesus did, the which, if they should be written every one, I suppose that even the world itself could not contain the books that should be written** (John 21:25). The Spirit of God must have given John that thought because he wrote as he was moved on by the Holy Ghost.

The Bible is a Holy Ghost book, and holy men of old wrote it as they were moved upon by the Holy Ghost. **For the prophecy came not in old time by the will of man: but holy men of God spake as they were moved by the Holy Ghost** (II Peter 1:21). They spake with power as they were moved on by the Holy Ghost. He is a person; and the Holy

Ghost power moved on them, and they wrote as they were moved on by that power so that every word was divine. The Bible did not come through the mind or the will of man; it came through the will of the Spirit. Therefore, since the Holy Spirit gave it, He can certainly explain it.

A DIVINE, INTELLIGENT PERSON

For there to be intelligent speech, there has to be an intelligent person behind it; so on the Day of Pentecost, there had to have been someone else doing the speaking. The disciples did not know all of those languages, so they could not have spoken them; and they were not being taught by somebody to speak in tongues. There had to have been an intelligent being behind the speech that was coming forth from their mouths.

When the Holy Ghost speaks through me, I know who is doing the speaking; and I know it is not me. When I am in prayer and meditation with the Lord, the Holy Ghost will take over my tongue and speak in many languages and dialects because I give Him a holy tongue that He can use; and it is always thrilling to me.

I delight in the Holy Spirit and in being alone with Him; He is great company. Some people talk about being so lonely and blue, and they think they have to be with people all the time; but God is calling you away to Himself. He wants to deal with you, to work with you and to show you His love. The Lord does not always want somebody else to tell you He loves you; He wants to tell you Himself. When divinity is in you, through you and with you, you will have that fellowship and the reality of God's greatness.

When Jesus came to Earth, He was a presence; but He was more than that—He was a person people could see. When the Holy Ghost came, He was a person, too; but He was invisible. The Lord said to the disciples, **I will pray the Father, and he shall give you another Comforter, that he may abide with you forever; Even the Spirit of truth; whom the world cannot receive, because it seeth him not, neither knoweth him: but ye know him; for he dwelleth with you, and shall be in you** (John 14:16,17). The disciples were going to have an intelligent person living on the inside of them who would teach them just like Jesus Himself did.

THE ELEMENTS OF SPEECH

How does speech come about? You first have a thought; then you receive understanding of that thought, and the third step is speech. You must also be familiar with the language you are going to speak in—you must have the thought in that language, the understanding in that language, and then you must be able to speak in that language. The Scriptures prove that this is right in I Corinthians where Paul explains the way speech is given to us. **When I was a child, I spake as a child, I understood as a child, I thought as a child: but when I became a man, I put away childish things** (I Corinthians 13:11).

Paul was describing his understanding in his childhood, but there was a purpose for it. By reversing the order of what Paul said, we can see the order in which speech works. First is the thought; next is the understanding, and then there is speech. It is a known fact that we think various thoughts on a subject. Next, by a process of analysis and summary, we come to an understanding or comprehension of it; and then we speak.

The disciples did not follow these steps at Pentecost. They spoke in unfamiliar languages; so they could not have had a thought, understood that thought or spoken it because you cannot do that in a language you don't know. Pentecost shows the miraculous speaking with tongues. It was miraculous then, and it still is today.

When the Lord spoke through Balaam's mule, was that God-talk or mule-talk? **And the LORD opened the mouth of the ass, and she said unto Balaam, What have I done unto thee, that thou hast smitten me these three times** (Numbers 22:28)? That was God-talk because the Lord was really speaking through that mule. However, when you are speaking in tongues at will, it is plain, old mule-talk, meaning it is just self.

Now, if God could use a dumb mule to speak through, should He not be able to give such a wonderful experience from Heaven to a gloriously saved person, one who is born of the Spirit of God, sanctified holy through the blood of the Lamb, has a holy tongue and holy hands to go with it and who is reaching up to receive?

THE SPIRIT MUST HAVE THE TONGUE

When you are seeking the baptism, the last thing you give over to the Lord is your tongue. That is why some of you make it so hard—you are trying to figure out how you can ever give your tongue over to Him when all you have to do is praise God. As I have already told you, when I was seeking for the Holy Ghost, I knew He was real; but I could not believe He would take over my tongue. I told the Lord, "You know I do not doubt your Word, but I doubt me being able to believe and accept that you will take over my tongue."

In spite of all that, I never stopped seeking; and one night, it happened. I was crying, "Glory, glory, glory!" and I didn't care what was going on around me. After a while, it seemed like one "glory" was pushing another "glory." Then I got to the place where my tongue was not saying "glory" quite right, and I just let it go. It was the Holy Ghost speaking, and He was saying words...and

He just went on and on. If He would stop, I would cry, "Glory!" a few more times; and He would start speaking again. How marvelous! It was so simple, and I had made it so hard. Of course, the devil will fight you and tell you that you are getting in the flesh; but, my God, that was where I had been living for eighteen years. The devil has no part in your baptism, so just wipe him out of your mind with the faith of God and go right on yielding.

If you are seeking the Holy Ghost, you need to get down to business. I would never let Heaven rest when I was seeking. I woke up saying, "Lord, give me the Holy Ghost." Before I went to sleep, I would say, "Lord, give me the Holy Ghost." I would walk down the street saying, "Lord, give me the Holy Ghost."

I was not interested in worldly music, newspapers, magazines or any books that man had written. I wanted the Holy Ghost, and there was only one book that told about it—the Bible. I read the Holy Scriptures, and I could not get enough of the second chapter of Acts where it tells of the disciples receiving the

Holy Ghost. I wanted that experience, and that was exactly what I got.

GIVE YOUR WHOLE SELF TO THE SPIRIT

No one can conquer the human tongue but the supernatural person of the Holy Spirit. You have to yield completely to Him and then stay yielded to Him so He can use you. When Jesus was here, He had eyes, ears, feet, hands and a tongue; but the Holy Ghost comes without any of those members. Neither does He dwell on the outside of you like Jesus did; He moves inside. Your hands become His hands; your feet become His feet, and your eyes become His eyes. Your mind becomes His mind to think through and to use to get things done, if you will give your mind over to Him.

If you give your mind over to the human spirit or let the enemy get in, you take it out of the Spirit's reach; so He has no power to feed you His thoughts or use your mind, and the Holy Ghost has to have your mind to be able to teach you. Sometimes, He works for hours or days to be able to teach people one tiny lesson; and even then, it may be crowded out in a matter of a few days by the enemy.

Then the weeds grow back in Eden.

You have to give your whole self to the Holy Spirit—give Him your body to be His temple and your mind for Him to work with. The Bible tells us, **Let this mind be in you, which was also in Christ Jesus** (Philippians 2:5). You come into one mind and one accord with divinity by taking on the mind of Christ.

God gave me 141 ingredients that made up the mind of Christ when He was here on Earth, and they are all explained to you in my book *The Mind of Christ*. The Bible tells us that we can add to the spiritual things we already have. **And beside this, giving all diligence, add to your faith virtue; and to virtue knowledge; And to knowledge temperance; and to temperance patience; and to patience godliness; And to godliness brotherly kindness; and to brotherly kindness charity** [love] (II Peter 1:5–7). We can add to our minds until we have the whole mind of Christ; and with that mind, the Holy Spirit can do His best work.

The Holy Spirit used Jesus' mind, His eyes and His voice; and the Holy Spirit has to use our voices, too. Jesus was divinity, yet He laid aside everything to become a man and to be a part of us. He became our elder brother and took on all the weaknesses of the flesh; and with the person of the Holy Spirit, He won, showing us that we can win, too. Without the Spirit, Jesus would not have won all of those victories as a human being.

Jesus had divine blood in His veins; and although we have only human blood in our veins, we have divine blood in our souls. When you receive the Lord, you have divinity in your soul; and your soul receives eternal life. If you keep that blood in your soul and never destroy it with sin, your soul will live forever; but if you sin against God, the blood no longer has any effect on you and disappears.

DRAWN AND DIRECTED BY THE SPIRIT

As a human being, Jesus had to be fed the Word; and the Holy Ghost feeds us the Word just as He fed Christ the Word. **Man shall not live by bread alone, but by every word that proceedeth out of the mouth of God** (Matthew 4:4).

You cannot get saved without the Holy Spirit because He is the one who convicts you and draws you. **No man can come to me, except the Father which hath sent me draw him: and I will raise him up at the last day** (John 6:44). The Holy Spirit is the agent in your born-again experience. He uses divine blood to wash away all of your sins and then seals your soul with the blood. The devil cannot get into your soul where the pure Word of God and all of the love, grace and goodness from the Lord are stored unless you commit a willful sin. Your soul is sealed with the blood; and no one can break that seal but you because it can only be broken from the inside, not from the outside.

If the Holy Spirit can use the blood to wash away all of your sins and seal your soul, why don't you trust Him with your mind? You have to yield to the Holy Spirit for Him to be able to use the blood again and again to cleanse your mind of the thoughts that the devil or people bring to you. If the mind was sealed off like the soul, the devil could not get to the mind and tempt you; however, there is a provision for the mind to be covered with the blood if you will use it...but you have to use it.

There is no need to keep wrestling with bad thoughts when the Holy Spirit will flush them right out with the things that Jesus brought just like you would flush the toilet. When you give your mind to the blood that is in your soul and to the Holy Spirit, He goes to work; and He gives you the beautiful thoughts of God.

Jesus brought everything we need, but we do not have the ability to use it all ourselves. The Holy Spirit is the one who has the ability to use it through us if we yield to Him. It is not within man to walk his own walk. The Bible tells us that a man's steps are directed by either a higher power or a lower power, the power of God or the power of the devil. **O LORD, I know that the way of man is not in himself: it is not in man that walketh to direct his steps** (Jeremiah 10:23).

You may be foolish enough to think that you can direct your own destiny, but you cannot; so you must decide which power is directing you. When the devil gets your attention, he brings worry, fretting, despair, oppression and depression. Such things are terrible, but you can be a child of God and still have all of those things in your mind. You may not be acting them out, but they are troubling you to death.

The Spirit works with power from On High on the inside of us, so you do not have to worry about the powers of darkness or the powers of people. Power from On High is the power above all other powers, and the Spirit knows just how to use it.

How much do you enjoy the Holy Spirit, and how happy are you in Him? If you have the person of the Holy Spirit living on the inside of you, you should be one of the happiest people on the Earth today. The Spirit came all the way from Heaven to move in and live with you; but because you cannot see Him, you do not recognize Him or believe He is a real person—not even after He has taken over your tongue, and you absolutely knew it was not you speaking.

THE SPIRIT REVEALS GOD'S WILL

The Holy Ghost prophesies, yet some people despise that when the Bible clearly tells us to

despise not prophesyings (I Thessalonians 5:20). They do not want anything foretold about their lives, and they don't want to hear that judgment might fall upon them.

The Holy Spirit reveals the whole will of God for our lives, yet so many people struggle to find the will of God because either they are mixing with the wrong people or struggling with the wrong things. They need to yield to the Holy Spirit and stay with Him until they know the mind of the Spirit for them. We have to be completely yielded to Him, and it is awful when people do not want to yield to God.

If you are not willing to do anything for the Lord, you will never get the whole will of God. Why?—because if you do not really want His will, you are not going to walk in it until you decide to yield to the Spirit. You may not want to do something God wants you to in your own spirit; but when you want God's will, you will give over to the Holy Spirit. Then you will come to the place where you will delight in doing the will of the Lord.

Jesus came to do the will of the Lord, but

He did not start His ministry until He had received the Holy Ghost; and the Holy Ghost is to be your helper, too. Never try to fast without His help or pray without Him being with you. You should always be conscious of Him, the One who brings you boldly before the throne of grace. **Let us therefore come boldly unto the throne of grace, that we may obtain mercy, and find grace to help in time of need** (Hebrews 4:16).

You can go boldly before the Lord through the Spirit of truth. When you have Him and you yield 100 percent to Him, you have all the favor of Heaven; and everything you need is available to you and even more through the Spirit of truth. We can be so close to the Lord because we have been made close through the blood. **But now in Christ Jesus ye who sometimes were far off are made nigh by the blood of Christ** (Ephesians 2:13).

KNOW WHAT THE SPIRIT CAN DO

The Bible tells us, **Not by might, nor by power, but by my spirit, saith the LORD of hosts** (Zechariah 4:6). Not by the might of man do we look for our physical strength and power; we look for them through the Holy Spirit. And where do we look?—on the inside of us. That is the first place you must look because the Holy Spirit cannot be a great help to you unless He is in there.

Do you ever wonder why God does not move for you more than He does? If you have what you should in your soul, then it is because you are not yielding to the Holy Spirit so He can use those things. You are tying your own hands, and the Spirit cannot use them. When you tie your own hands and stop up your own ears, you are in trouble.

We have to yield to the Spirit in truth to know He is the Spirit of truth, and then He will draw us into the things of God. He is the keeper of our lives, and He keeps us in contact with Heaven and in the unity of Heaven. He keeps the lines clear for us if we live holy, and He takes us right into that most holy place before the throne of God. He keeps us in unity with angels, and angels will work more and more for you if you will yield to the Spirit like you should all the time.

The Holy Spirit has to prepare you, but He

has a time getting some of us ready to go in before the throne of grace so we can find help. All of our grumbling, complaining, fretting and doubting have to go. The Spirit keeps working and working, and He helps to dress the whole you in all of the armor of God. Then He teaches you the value of that divine armor, but some people do not know what the armor is or what it consists of let alone the value of it.

Wherefore take unto you the whole armour of God, that ye may be able to withstand in the evil day, and having done all, to stand. Stand therefore, having your loins girt about with truth, and having on the breastplate of righteousness; And your feet shod with the preparation of the gospel of peace; Above all, taking the shield of faith, wherewith ye shall be able to quench all the fiery darts of the wicked. And take the helmet of salvation, and the sword of the Spirit, which is the word of God (Ephesians 6:13–17).

BE CONSCIOUS OF THE SPIRIT

Are you in the truth today? If so, the Holy Spirit will help you get ready for every day you have left. Do you depend on Him to help dress you in the spiritual things you will need for each day and to get you ready to go forth? If you go forth only half ready, the devil may win part of the victory over you that day. You must go forth fully dressed by the Holy Spirit. He will give you all you need for each day, and He will serve it to you in abundance.

How conscious are you of the Spirit's holy presence? I am so conscious of His presence; He gives me a feeling of such holy sacredness, and it affects all of my flesh. He has the power to take you and me right into the very presence of God; and through the blood, He is able to do it—but you must accept the blood. Then you must get quiet. The Lord said, **Be still, and know that I am God** (Psalm 46:10). In other words, "Be still and feel me. Feel my presence and my holiness and righteousness. Breathe my grace." The spiritual man breathes the graces of the Lord.

Feel that holy sacredness of knowing that

the invisible person lives with you. It does not matter what is going on around you because you cannot control all of that, but you can be concerned about the invisible person who has come to live with you day and night until the Rapture takes place or death causes you to go home.

We are so conscious of people. A person can get your attention just by walking up to you, but what does the Holy Spirit have to do to get your attention? He has to have it because He cannot teach you anything unless He has your attention. He cannot direct your steps without making you conscious of where you are stepping, and He cannot reveal truth to you unless He can get your mind; but how much trouble does He have getting your mind? He dwells in the body, but He has to have the mind; and you must be conscious of that. May God help us to accept Him in living reality today.

I asked the Lord to help me make His Holy Spirit so real to you. I want you to feel His presence like I do. As a child of God, you know you are set apart; but I want you to get into His presence so there will be times when you will feel that presence of being set apart. You may know you are living holy; but I want you to sense that holiness in your flesh and in your Spirit, in your brain, your eyes and your ears. I am trying to get you to be conscious of the Holy Spirit in the way He wants you to be conscious of Him. You must hear the Holy Spirit.

Many of you are always looking for something, but you do not know what it is. Let the Holy Spirit teach you what it is. He is there with such power, and all nine gifts of the Spirit belong to Him so He can use those gifts for humanity and for the body of Christ.

This invisible person of such strength, power and intelligence is so valuable; yet how much intelligence do people give Him credit for when they say, "We do not believe He speaks; we do not believe in tongues"? How can anybody expect to get into Heaven and deny the tongue of the Holy Spirit? You cannot even be saved without the Holy Spirit because He has to be the one who uses the blood on your soul. You can only use the blood by faith; and when you do, that gives the Spirit the liberty to actually use the blood for you in all of its power to cleanse you and to wash away your sins.

People are not going to be able to deny God's power in this last hour. *And you are going to have to have the Holy Ghost to get out of here, saith the Lord.* You will not make the Rapture without His baptism. You can say you don't believe that, but it does not matter what you believe. The Bible says, **Let God be true, but every man a liar** (Romans 3:4). You must have the Holy Ghost.

THE SPIRIT IS BEING POURED OUT

The Holy Ghost is big and mighty, so let Him be big in your life. Stop looking at yourself and start looking at Him. Look for Him in the Holy Bible, and you will find Him in all the truth of God. He knows man, and He knows you and me. He was in Eden when the perfect man was made, and Adam was perfect in every way. The Spirit wants to operate in the same perfection through those of us who are without sin and have a holy tongue, holy eyes and holy ears. Man had perfect control in Eden; and through the Holy Spirit, you can, too. However, when man left Eden and the shelter of God, it was a disaster. Very few people were totally yielded to God in Old Testament days, and there were such a few whom God could really pour Himself into and through.

We are now in the last hour, and this dispensation of the Holy Ghost is about to end. The Holy Ghost is being poured out now, so why haven't some of you received Him? Answer that question for yourself and nobody else. For some of you, it is not because there is sin or disobedience in your heart; it is because you do not know how to give over to Him. Others of you have received Him, but you do not know how to yield to Him in everything so that He can really serve you all that you need. You go lacking again and again spiritually, physically and financially because you do not know how to receive. He cannot fulfill His promises for you or serve you from those promises if you are not ready for Him to serve them to you.

If you are not on the receiving side of the table, the Holy Spirit cannot serve you. He could put it out there; but when you are on the wrong side of the table, you are not going to reach for it. Only those on the receiving side can partake of it and receive. You see other people being blessed and wonder, "Why can't I receive like that? Why can't I be close to God and get answers to my prayers?" You can! Say as Paul said, **For I know whom I have believed, and am persuaded that he is able to keep that which I have committed unto him against that day** (II Timothy 1:12).

CHAPTER **6**

Conditions for Receiving the Holy Spirit

Now that you know who the Holy Ghost is and that He is promised to all who obey Him, you also must know how to receive Him. All of God's promises are conditional, and knowing the conditions for receiving the Holy Ghost is so important for those who are seeking Him as well as for those who are helping others to receive the baptism. If people will meet the seven conditions given in this chapter, they will receive the Holy Ghost and not come up lacking...and it will be the same Holy Ghost baptism that the disciples received on the Day of Pentecost.

GOD PROMISED WE COULD RECEIVE

The gift of the Holy Spirit is given and received, and it is as much of a promise as is the promise of salvation; but again, God's promises are conditional. The Bible says that if we repent, the Lord will forgive. **If we confess our sins, he is faithful and just to forgive us our sins, and to cleanse us from all unrighteousness** (I John 1:9). It also says we must repent with godly sorrow. **For godly sorrow worketh repentance to salvation not to be repented of** (II Corinthians 7:10). Godly sorrow is being as sorry for the sins you have committed as God is that you committed them. Until you are sorry for your sins with godly sorrow, you are not sorry enough to reach repentance from Heaven.

But when the fulness of the time was come, God sent forth his Son, made of a woman, made under the law, To redeem them that were under the law, that we might receive the adoption of sons (Galatians 4:4,5). We receive the adoption of sons by receiving Christ and believing that He has given us the right to become sons of God according to His promise. **But as many as received him, to them gave he power to become the sons of God, even to them that believe on his name** (John 1:12).

Jesus told the people that if they believed, they would become sons of God; and they did. In the same way, He is giving us the right to receive the Holy Ghost and to become sons and daughters endued with Holy Ghost power...and it all comes through Jesus Christ.

You should definitely enjoy receiving the Spirit, and you should anticipate the baptism from the moment you get saved. After God saved me, I could not wait to receive the Holy Ghost; and I was determined not to put it off. I didn't go to man; I looked to Heaven day and night because I knew that was where the Holy Ghost would come from. I was running after the Lord for one thing—the baptism of power, the baptism of the Spirit of truth, the baptism of the Holy Ghost.

Now, we will begin looking at the conditions indicated in the Holy Scriptures by which the Holy Spirit is given and received.

CONDITION NUMBER ONE:
FORGIVENESS

On the Day of Pentecost, Peter said, **Repent, and be baptized every one of you in the name of Jesus Christ for the remission of sins, and ye shall receive the gift of the Holy Ghost** (Acts 2:38). You have to receive forgiveness from God; but to receive that forgiveness, you have to forgive. You cannot carry the forgiveness of God in your spirit and be ready to get the Holy Ghost if you have not forgiven your enemies and people who have done you wrong. The Lord said He would forgive us as we forgive others. **For if ye forgive men their trespasses, your heavenly Father will also forgive you: But if ye forgive not men their trespasses, neither will your Father forgive your trespasses** (Matthew 6:14,15).

If you have not fully forgiven others, you are not eligible for the baptism of the Holy Ghost because the blood has to cleanse the temple of every particle of sin before you can be baptized. Without divine blood, the Spirit will never move in because the temple can never be clean enough without it.

When Christ dealt with the temple in Jerusalem, the first thing He did was to cleanse it. **And Jesus went into the temple of God, and cast out all them that sold and bought in the temple, and overthrew the tables of the moneychangers, and the seats of them that sold doves, And said unto them, It is written, My house shall be called the house of prayer; but ye have made it a den of thieves** (Matthew 21:12,13).

Many people have received the Spirit without being baptized in water but not without forgiveness for their souls. You cannot have the Holy Ghost until you are saved, and you are not saved until you are forgiven of every sin. You must have complete deliverance from sin or your soul is not accepted in the eyes of God here on Earth or in Heaven.

The Holy Dove cannot dwell among unclean birds, so to speak. He only comes in when all of the unclean birds and the mess they have made in the soul have been washed away, and nothing can cleanse a soul but the blood of Jesus. Some, however, deny the divinity of

Christ and the precious blood of Jesus; but that is despising the testimony of the Holy Spirit and insulting Him to His face, and multitudes are doing that today. **Who hath trodden under foot the Son of God, and hath counted the blood...an unholy thing, and hath done despite unto the Spirit of grace** [the Spirit of truth] (Hebrews 10:29).

It is terrible when people despise the blood and the divinity of Christ because those who do without the blood have to do without the Spirit; and without the Spirit, there is no way to Heaven. The Spirit of truth is the one who connects you with Calvary so you can receive salvation and with divinity so you can receive the Holy Ghost baptism. He also connects you with Heaven so you can get prayers through.

CONDITION NUMBER TWO:
SONSHIP

When you become a son or daughter of God, He sends forth His Spirit into your heart. **And because ye are sons, God hath sent forth the Spirit of his Son into your hearts, crying, Abba, Father** (Galatians 4:6). Every son and daughter should resemble his or her father, so God sends the Holy Spirit forth into our hearts to live and dwell so that people might be changed into His image through that Spirit. **But we all, with open face beholding as in a glass the glory of the Lord, are changed into the same image from glory to glory, even as by the Spirit of the Lord** (II Corinthians 3:18). The Holy Spirit washes away the sins of the soul with divine blood, and the Holy Spirit changes us into the image of the Father. Had it not been for Adam and Eve's fall, we all would have been born in that image.

It is one thing to claim to be a son or daughter of God but quite another thing to claim the likeness of Him, and the likeness is the outward evidence of that relationship. If you are not in the likeness of Jesus, the only begotten Son, you are not in the likeness of the Father.

Jesus said, **He that hath seen me hath seen the Father** (John 14:9). As sons and daughters of God, we should be able to say the same thing to a lost world. We must act like Jesus, talk like Jesus, think like Jesus, walk like Jesus, work like Jesus and believe like Jesus. That likeness must show up on the outside of you as evidence that you have that relationship with God. If it does not show on the outside, you do not have it; and there is no need to say or pretend that you do. There are too many pretenders in the world today who are not genuine children of God. We must want to have that daughter or son relationship with God, and you have to meet that condition to receive the Holy Ghost baptism.

CONDITION NUMBER THREE:
FEELING THE NEED

You have to feel the need of not being able to go on without the Holy Spirit. Even Jesus Himself, the very Son of God, knew He had to have the Holy Ghost before He could start His ministry; and He did receive Him. John the Baptist saw the Spirit descending on Jesus in the form of a dove. **And John bare record, saying, I saw the Spirit descending from heaven like a dove, and it abode upon him** (John 1:32). Later, Jesus said, **The Spirit of the Lord is upon me, because he hath anointed me to preach the gospel to the poor; he hath sent me to heal the**

brokenhearted, to preach deliverance to the captives, and recovering of sight to the blind, to set at liberty them that are bruised (Luke 4:18).

When you know that you have to have the Holy Ghost, you will get down to business. **For I will pour water upon him that is thirsty, and floods upon the dry ground** (Isaiah 44:3). The Lord will pour water upon whom?—the seeker. The water of the Spirit will be his, but the person has to be thirsty and want it. If you are not really thirsty for the baptism, you are not likely to receive.

He giveth power to the faint (Isaiah 40:29). God will pour forth His floods of miracle water from On High upon those who seek the Holy Ghost as people dying of thirst, but those who think they can live without Him are not likely to receive. The enemy is deceiving you when you feel like you can live without the Holy Ghost and make it on what you have. Just because you have the lamp of salvation and you have some light, you think you will make it; but you won't make it without the Holy Ghost.

We have so much in store for us in this

final hour but not without the Holy Spirit. I pity you who don't have the greatness of the Spirit because you will have great sorrows like you have never had before, and you will regret not receiving the Spirit. *If you were really saved, saith the Lord, you would want the Holy Ghost; and you would want the fullness of the Spirit.* If you do not want the Holy Ghost, you are not really saved; and you must realize it. If you were to die today, you would go to hell. *You are deceived, saith the Lord;* and I must tell you that you are. Now, that does not mean that you will go to hell if you are saved and die without the baptism; but if you are really saved, you will be seeking to receive that holy baptism.

If you are not seeking, you are stubborn and rebellious and far away from God. You are in a lukewarm condition, and He is getting ready to spew you out of His mouth into the Tribulation Period. How sad. **I know thy works, that thou art neither cold nor hot: I would thou wert cold or hot. So then because thou art lukewarm, and neither cold nor hot, I will spue thee out of my mouth**

(Revelation 3:15,16). You who are lukewarm belong to the world church, whether you realize it or not; and the Lord is doing everything He can to shake you up.

You can make yourself hungry by thinking about food all the time, and you can make your soul thirsty by thinking about the Holy Ghost all the time. If you do not have Him, you should think more about Him than you do about sleeping, eating or anything else. You must feel the need of the Holy Ghost more than you do food. You must feel the need of Him enough to give Him your time and a day for Him to move in, and you must hold the door open for Him until He comes in. I was willing to do anything to receive the Holy Ghost because I knew I just had to have Him.

Today, even Pentecostal preachers are telling people they do not have to have the Holy Ghost to make the Rapture, but they are among the foolish virgins we have already studied in Matthew 25:1–13. They are making their congregations to be full of foolish virgins; and soon, they will find that they don't have the oil. Then it will be too late for them to get it just like it was for the five foolish virgins.

DO NOT WAIT TOO LONG

Now is the time to get the oil of the Spirit; and if you are actually looking for Jesus to come, you will definitely feel the need of it. The devil will tell you that you have plenty of time, but you don't; and one day, there will be no time left. The very last moment of countdown time will come, and you will have no Holy Ghost, no oil.

How tragic to have the Gospel light and be in the mouth of God only to be spewed out into the Tribulation Period as a reject from the one flight out. You may really seek God then and make Him all kinds of promises, and you may tarry for days and nights to get the Holy Ghost; but you will not receive Him.

When the Bride leaves here, nobody else will receive the gift of the Spirit because the Holy Ghost dispensation will be closed; and He will be as far from you as Earth is from Heaven. You will think, "What a fool I was not to feel the need of that oil!" You had better feel the need of it today because soon it will be too late. I believed I had to have the Holy Ghost to make the Rapture; so after I was saved, I felt the need of the Spirit, and I wasted no time in seeking God day and night until I had received the baptism.

If you have the Holy Ghost, you must feel the need of others receiving Him. At the church where I received the Holy Ghost, altar workers would gather around the seekers; and they did not give up on them. If people got discouraged, the altar workers prayed it right out of them and kept them praising God. They would encourage people to try one more time, and I saw them pray so many people through who had decided to try one more time. If you don't think you can be an altar worker, then you need to change.

Those who helped me receive worked as hard as if they had been seeking the baptism for themselves. Many of those dear, old saints of God are in Heaven now, and I sure do want to meet them one day. I believe with all of my heart that they will share in the reward of all the souls who have been and will be won through this Jesus ministry.

The Lord never promised to pour this great, heavenly water upon anyone who is not thirsty. He is ready to pour the water only on thirsty ground, and we cry for that thirsty ground to be watered all around us and in nations around the world. That is why in our crusade services, thousands of people receive the Holy Ghost as He falls. They see the miracles of God; and when I tell them that they come through the power of the Holy Ghost, it makes them thirsty.

CONDITION NUMBER FOUR:
FAITH

Christ hath redeemed us from the curse of the law, being made a curse for us: for it is written, Cursed is every one that hangeth on a tree: That the blessing of Abraham might come on the Gentiles through Jesus Christ; that we might receive the promise of the Spirit through faith (Galatians 3:13,14). This verse says that Christ hath redeemed us, and you cannot get salvation or the Holy Ghost without faith. Jesus said, **Only believe** (Mark 5:36).

Down through the years, some preachers

have taught people that they did not have to receive a baptism of the Spirit. They have said that people could just take the Spirit by faith with no evidence of speaking in tongues according to Acts 2:4, but that means taking nothing at all. When the disciples were baptized on the Day of Pentecost, the Spirit took them over and gave them a real tongue of fire.

When we meet the conditions of God's promise for receiving the baptism of the Holy Ghost, all hell cannot keep us from being baptized. Your family can't keep you from being baptized; and even if all your enemies on Earth were gathered around at one time, they could not keep you from being baptized. All Heaven is for you, and Heaven is the strongest power there is. When Heaven comes down, the devils have to flee.

I want to go back to Galatians 3:13,14 and make it very clear to you. It first states a fact: *Christ hath redeemed us.* Then it declares the purpose for that fact: *that we might receive the promise of the Spirit.* If you have been redeemed, why do you hesitate in accepting this purpose? You receive it through faith, a gift from God; and God's gift of divine faith works.

CONDITION NUMBER FIVE:
OBEDIENCE

And we are his witnesses of these things; and so is also the Holy Ghost, whom God hath given to them that obey him (Acts 5:32). Do you obey the Lord in everything? Obedience counts whether you need a miracle for your body, for your finances or for your soul. When the Lord said He would give the Holy Ghost to them that obey Him, He meant those who will cooperate with Him; and you will only receive that spirit of cooperation through obedience.

Everything comes through obedience, and the obedient shall receive the best of God from Heaven. **If ye be willing and obedient, ye shall eat the good of the land** (Isaiah 1:19). The heavens will open for the obedient, but you can be disobedient to God and refuse to see that you are when you are living by your opinions and the opinions of others who agree with you.

Years ago, I was conducting services in the mountains of Kentucky; and one night after service, the pastor asked me to go with him to visit a man who was said to be dying. I had just closed a big service in which I had given all I had, and I didn't feel like climbing a mountain; but, of course, I agreed. It seemed like we hiked and hiked, and I was so tired; but we finally got up there.

When we knelt down to pray, a laughing spirit came over me; and I just wanted to laugh and laugh. The man declared he was dying, but I couldn't pray without laughing to save my life. It was a good thing the other pastor was really praying because I didn't want any of the family to see me. What would they think if they saw me laughing? Then all of a sudden, the man blurted out, "Lord, if you will heal me, I'll pay my tithes!" He got well immediately; and I thought, "No wonder I wanted to laugh; God was laughing through me because that rotten fellow would not pay his tithes."

I was disgusted as I walked back down that mountain, and I don't know whether or not that man ever paid his tithes; but I was never called on to pray for him again.

BE OBEDIENT IN ALL THINGS

Are you giving God His part when it comes to your finances? If not, you are robbing Him. He told His chosen people, **Will a man rob God? Yet ye have robbed me. But ye say, Wherein have we robbed thee? In tithes and offerings** (Malachi 3:8). Some people think that tithing was only required under the Law. If it was, then how much more important is it for us to pay tithes under grace? Jesus said to the Pharisees, This **ought ye to have done** [tithe]**, and not to leave the other undone** (Matthew 23:23). The Pharisees tithed every little thing and were so pious about it, but they did not live holy.

You cannot just tithe and expect to go to Heaven; you have to be born again. You will be rewarded for your works and for your tithing and giving. If you really love God with your whole heart, He will be the last person you will cheat on anything. When you shortchange God, it causes Him to shortchange you; and then you cry, "God, why are you treating me like this?" But you really know why.

Your willingness and readiness to do God's

will mean everything when you are seeking the baptism of the Holy Ghost. You will never get any closer to Heaven without actually putting your feet on the streets of gold than you are when the Holy Ghost comes in. He has you completely; and there is no poison, gossip or criticism in your tongue. Your opinions are all gone, and your tongue is as holy as God's tongue is; so the Holy Spirit can use it as His very own tongue.

ANYTHING FOR GOD

Are you ready to do all of God's will, or do you just say that you are? Are you willing to do anything God wants you to do, or do you complain when He puts you in a certain place to do something for His work? If you do, that is not obedience; it is arrogance and rebellion. I have never complained about any work I have had to do for the Lord. From the time God saved me, I would scrub a floor, dig a ditch and do anything for Jesus; and I have always looked at it as work for Jesus.

Man did not call me to preach; God called me to preach, and He never discussed finances with me. I never thought about how I would get along out in the world. I did not have people supporting me, and there were no preachers in my family; so how did I make it?—through faith. Many years ago, I adopted the phrase, "I will make it; I always make it!" That phrase means that God always brings me out. When the going would get rough, I would say it; and I really needed it.

If you are not ready and willing to do anything God wants you to do no matter how humble the task, you are not ready for the Holy Ghost. However, if you are ready to do anything God wants you to do, then you can expect the help of the Holy Ghost; and you can expect Him to come into your life to stay. If there is any disobedience in your heart, you must not let the devil deceive you about it. These conditions are not just to get the Holy Ghost to move in but to really keep Him there.

CONDITION NUMBER SIX: *WAITING*

Jesus told the disciples to wait, and they would receive; but they would have to believe. **Tarry...until ye be endued with power from on high** (Luke 24:49). Tarry means "to stay."

What if the Lord would one day tell candidates for the Holy Ghost, "You must stay in my house until you get the Holy Ghost"? What if an angel would suddenly appear and say, "The Lord is coming in thirty minutes"? I am sure every person would pray through to the Holy Ghost whether anybody helped them or not, and even sinners would get saved and receive the Holy Ghost. We all must check our oil of the Spirit daily, and I am always ordering up more.

When you tarry until, you wait for the promise of the Father. **And, being assembled together with them,** [Jesus] **commanded them that they should not depart from Jerusalem, but wait for the promise of the Father, which, saith he, ye have heard of me** (Acts 1:4). When you are waiting for the promise of the Father, you don't run home, leave to do something else or think about feeding your stomach; you hunger and thirst after righteousness, and the Holy Ghost is righteousness. The disciples waited, and the filling came—they were filled with the Holy Ghost.

God does not go by our watches, and we

shouldn't either if we are going to go deep with Him. When God saved me, I was anxious to be with Him; and unless I had to do something urgent, I paid no attention to my watch. I was on Heaven's clock, and I was on time with God day and night.

There are some who interpret Luke 24:49 and Acts 1:4 as *work until you are endued with power*, and *work for the promise of the Father*. The Lord didn't say *work*; He said *wait*. You can't work for the promise of the Father to be fulfilled in your life, and you can't work until He gives you power from On High. You have to wait, but many are afraid to do that just in case all would go wrong. God can do without their restlessness, and that is exactly what it is. They wonder, "Why don't I get the Holy Ghost? I see other people who are receiving, so I wonder if they are getting the real thing. I don't know why God doesn't give me the baptism when I pray, live good and go to church." God is telling you why in this book.

CONDITION NUMBER SEVEN:
YOUR PRAYER LIFE

The heavenly Father will give the Holy Spirit to those who ask Him; but if your prayer life is not right, you cannot ask Him in the right way. Jesus said, **If ye abide in me, and my words abide in you, ye shall ask what ye will, and it shall be done unto you** (John 15:7).

Prayer is exciting, so stop doubting in your prayer time. When you are full of the Holy Ghost, you can say as Christ did, **Father, I thank thee that thou hast heard me. And I knew that thou hearest me always** (John 11:41,42). That will really build your faith in a great way. God is busy on His throne, but He always takes time to listen to me. I have no room for doubt, so why don't you call on Him like that? It works for me, and it will work for you.

Prayer is not words; prayer is faith and love, and it was while Jesus was praying that the heavens opened and the Holy Ghost descended. **Now when all the people were baptized, it came to pass, that Jesus also being baptized, and praying, the heaven**

was opened, And the Holy Ghost descended in a bodily shape like a dove upon him, and a voice came from heaven, which said, Thou art my beloved Son; in thee I am well pleased (Luke 3:21,22).

Jesus had told the disciples that He would pray to the Father, and He would send the Comforter; and that was exactly what happened. See what prayer will do? The Son of God prayed, and He made it possible for many thirsty sons and daughters of God to be ready to be filled. However, of all the great multitudes who met Jesus and received fabulous miracles—some even had their dead raised—only about 120 went to the Upper Room. **The number of names together were about an hundred and twenty** (Acts 1:15).

Only about 120 people met the seven conditions that would enable them to go to the Upper Room, but there should have been thousands there. Five hundred saw Jesus at one time after He had been resurrected. **He was seen of above five hundred brethren at once; of whom the greater part remain unto this present, but some are fallen asleep**

(I Corinthians 15:6). Where were those 500 that day, and where are "the 500" today who have received great miracles from God? They are not going on into the greatness of the Lord when Heaven paid such a great price.

Prayer brought the glory of God down even in Old Testament days. **Now when Solomon had made an end of praying...the glory of the LORD filled the house** (II Chronicles 7:1). When the people in the Upper Room had made an end of praying, the glory filled their tabernacles of clay. They became temples of the Holy Ghost, and the Holy Ghost moved into their houses of clay that had been cleansed by the blood of the Lamb.

MEET THE CONDITIONS

God is not an unreasonable God. He said, **Come now, and let us reason together** (Isaiah 1:18); and He wants to reason with you. Why should He give you someone as valuable as the third person in the Trinity of the Godhead if you do not value Him? The person of the Holy Ghost will walk right into your life and into your innermost being to baptize you, but some people doubt the Holy

Spirit because they will not let Him become a reality to them. I did not doubt the Holy Spirit when He came in because I was looking for Him, and I recognized Him.

Let us review these seven conditions: forgiveness, sonship, feeling the need, faith, obedience, waiting, prayer. You who are candidates for the baptism must meet these qualifications. You have to go through or you will still be here after the Rapture has taken place and wish you had gotten ready. Jesus said, **Therefore be ye also ready: for in such an hour as ye think not the Son of man cometh** (Matthew 24:44); and to be ready, you must have the oil of the Spirit in your lamp.

Anybody can get the Holy Ghost if he will meet these seven conditions, and there are even more conditions than these; but if you will keep these seven in mind, they will help you. If you already have the Holy Ghost, you can use them to help somebody else; and you can also use them to give the Holy Ghost more freedom in your life. You can't be in and out with the Spirit; you have to be yielded to Him and to the will of the Father.

Faith is all you need today, but are you going after houses and lands more than you are the Holy Ghost or the lost? Souls are waiting for you to get to them with the Gospel light and the message of Jesus Christ.

The Lord is getting us ready for the world outreach. He started me on my journey to the world as just a little country boy who had never been even 100 miles from home; and if a little country boy could start on such a journey, it should give you the faith to know that you can make the journey to the ends of the Earth, too.

The Bible cannot just be under your arm; it must also be in your heart so you can pour it out to people wherever you go. You must be familiar with God's Word so that you will not miss one soul. You never know when someone will ask you a question about God, and it all depends on how you answer that question as to whether that soul will be won or lost. There are times when just giving part of the answer or the wrong answer will cause you to lose a soul; and I am sure all Heaven cries over that.

BE READY TO GO

The Lord is drawing on you to get you ready to get out of here; and when the Holy Ghost makes His final sweep, you are going to have to be connected with Him. There will be no time to make anything right, no time to ask anybody to forgive you and no time to get rid of a grudge. When the Holy Ghost takes His flight, it will be just like He is gathering all of us at one time into His arms; and we will be changed in a moment and in a twinkling of an eye.

Only the Holy Ghost can dress us in the robes of righteousness and holiness that we must be dressed in to get the job done that God has for us to do and to be the glorious Bride. The Lord said, **Thou art all fair, my love; there is no spot in thee** (Song of Solomon 4:7). The greatness of the Holy Spirit is beyond all of us, and we will never learn all about Him as the endless ages roll; but those of us who make it will be glad we had Him. I don't know how anybody can live without the Holy Ghost.

Now is the pouring-out time; and if you

don't accept the pouring out of the Spirit, you are going to be spewed into the Tribulation Period because you won't be a fit subject to be on the one flight out. You may think I don't know what I am talking about and that I am just trying to scare you. Well, I wish I could scare you, but you are beyond feeling. You should be alarmed about that, but you aren't. You may think you are pretty smart, but you are awfully dumb; and God wants you to know that.

The Spirit is preparing night and day for this great event called the Rapture, and He will be so jubilant when He meets Jesus in the air and presents the glorious Bride to Him. Do you know the Holy Ghost is the one who will present the Bride? He is here to get the Bride ready because the Lord is not coming all the way to Earth at His second appearance. He is coming in midair, and the Holy Ghost will present the Bride to Jesus there. **For the Lord himself shall descend from heaven with a shout, with the voice of the archangel, and with the trump of God: and the dead in Christ shall rise first: Then we which**

are alive and remain shall be caught up together with them in the clouds, to meet the Lord in the air: and so shall we ever be with the Lord (I Thessalonians 4:16,17).

Jesus will lead the spotless Bride right down the Avenue of Glory and present His loveable, beautiful Bride to the Father. That will be a glorious day! Won't you be glad that you paid the price and that you obeyed the Lord? Won't you be glad to stand before the Father without spot, wrinkle, blemish or any such thing? Won't you be glad to see the crowds of people from all over the world standing with you whom you helped bring into the Kingdom? When you think of Jesus and of Paul and of the price they paid, we are not really paying much of a price at all.

Today, the Bride is crying, **Draw me, we will run after thee** (Song of Solomon 1:4). We who are full of the Spirit today are being drawn by the greatness of His power, and we are running our last mile home. We are running after souls; but without the Holy Ghost, you will not have the vision of this hour or know what time it is in Heaven. Only through the Holy Ghost can you know what time it is. Heaven's clock is saying that it is almost midnight, the time for the one flight out; and we must be alert. We cannot be asleep like the disciples were before Pentecost.

MOVE ON IN WITH HIM

Years ago, God took me into the deep with Him. I had to be willing to die for His name's sake, but would I? We can tell the Lord we will, but we have to mean it. When I told the Lord I would die for His name's sake, He knew I meant it. I could have walked out and died for Him at any moment if it would have finished the work, but the Lord let me know that He had to use me to work for Him. However, I had to be in shape for the Lord to use me, and I had to let nothing stop me. Then it would not matter what people did to me or how much they fought me.

If you are not made of the real stuff in this final hour, you will not last; but if you are standing as tall as Jesus stood and in the unity of the Spirit with God's people, nothing can shake you out. We must be in one mind and one spirit and not want anybody around who criticizes God's work or what we are doing for Him. We must ask God to send us new people He can use to help us in our work, and He is doing just that. No matter who you are, what race you are, whether you are educated or uneducated, rich or poor, you are still loved by God.

We must live and dwell under the wings of the Almighty and take our place with Him. We cannot be afraid of this hour or of what is coming upon the Earth. We must know our destiny and in whom we have believed, and we must know He will keep us because He promised He would.

We must be happy because we are blessed and have nothing to fear and nothing to worry about. If you are obedient to the Lord and you lose your job, He promised to look out for you and to supply your needs. Take on the spirit of humility from Jesus, and you will be all right in everything.

CHAPTER 7

What Does It Mean to Be Full of the Holy Ghost?

Is there a difference between being filled and being full of the Holy Ghost? According to the Bible, there is a drastic difference; and this chapter will reveal that difference to you.

Why does the Lord say only in some places that people were "full of the Holy Ghost"?—because all who receive the baptism are filled, but all are not full. It is possible to be baptized in the Holy Ghost and yet not be full of Him. The Lord let me know that being full of the Spirit means yielding to all the Lord is telling us so He can do all He wants to do in us and through us. Then He will be able to do whatever He wants on a massive scale to bring in the harvest.

When you are full of the Spirit, He makes God real, Jesus real and Himself real; so you have the fullness of the Godhead dwelling on the inside of you just as the Bible declares. **For in him dwelleth all the fulness of the Godhead bodily** (Colossians 2:9).

When you receive the Holy Ghost, He fills you up to the brim; but it is up to you to go beyond in order to become full and to stay full. Going beyond depends on your actions, the way you think, the way you believe and the way you accept divinity. It depends on your complete obedience—not to self but to the Lord—and on the way you yield in obedience to the Holy Spirit. Do you yield all the time or just part of the time?

When your stomach is filled up with food, it is happy; and in the same way, when your soul and mind are full of the Holy Ghost, it gives you a happy life in Jesus because you are just like Him. You make each step with His shoes on, and you walk just like He did.

Jesus said to the disciples, **Follow thou me** (John 21:22). Then He saw to it that they could receive the Holy Ghost and be full of the Spirit.

THE FIRE OF THE HOLY GHOST

To be full of the Holy Ghost is to be full of divine love, divine humility, the divine anointing and the good works of God all the time. You will have ears to hear what the Spirit is saying and eyes to see what the Lord wants you to see. You will have holy hands all the time which in turn means you will have a holy heart. You will have the divine sense of taste so that when the Holy Ghost feeds you the Word of God, you can taste and see that the Lord is good. **O taste and see that the LORD is good** (Psalm 34:8).

Being full of the Holy Ghost means you will have a heart of total obedience and one that is hot with the fire of the Holy Ghost. John said, **I indeed baptize you with water unto repentance: but he that cometh after me is mightier than I, whose shoes I am not worthy to bear: he shall baptize you with the Holy Ghost, and with fire** (Matthew 3:11).

Some teachers and preachers have taught that the fire John referred to is hellfire, but the Lord doesn't baptize us with hellfire; He baptizes us with the fire of the Holy Ghost. Study the Word of God which says, **For our God is a consuming fire** (Hebrews 12:29).

Jeremiah said it was like fire shut up in his bones. **But his word was in mine heart as a burning fire shut up in my bones** (Jeremiah 20:9). Isaiah the prophet received the tongue of fire, the Holy Ghost. **Then flew one of the seraphims unto me, having a live coal in his hand, which he had taken with the tongs from off the altar: And he laid it upon my mouth, and said, Lo, this hath touched thy lips; and thine iniquity is taken away, and thy sin purged. Also I heard the voice of the Lord, saying, Whom shall I send, and who will go for us? Then said I, Here am I; send me** (Isaiah 6:6–8). At first, Isaiah had rejected God's call because the people were rebellious, hardhearted and would not listen; but after he had received the tongue of fire, he said, "Here am I, Lord; send me." Suddenly, he was begging the Lord not to send anybody else.

The fire of the Holy Ghost appeared in the Old Testament again and again, and it showed up in the New Testament in a most vivid way on the Day of Pentecost. **And when the day of Pentecost was fully come, they were all with one accord in one place. And suddenly there came a sound from heaven as of a rushing mighty wind, and it filled all the house where they were sitting** (Acts 2:1,2). The mighty, rushing wind was not the evidence of the Holy Ghost; it was just a symbol of His greatness.

And there appeared unto them cloven tongues like as of fire, and it sat upon each of them (Acts 2:3). People saw those tongues of fire, and those who were filled and stayed full of the Holy Ghost kept a hot heart of spiritual fire beating in rhythm with the heart of God.

When you are full of the Holy Ghost, your heart matches the heart of God. His desire is your desire; His plans are your plans, and His way is your way. You are on fire for God; and you say, "Give me something to do for Jesus!" I was that way from the hour God saved me. I took on the mind of Christ; and when you have His mind, you will put Him first and want to please Him daily. You will forever seek His face with all of your heart, and your mind will be stayed upon the Lord. Then you will find peace of mind. **Thou wilt keep him in perfect peace, whose mind is stayed on thee: because he trusteth in thee** (Isaiah 26:3).

LED BY THE SPIRIT

When you are full of the Holy Ghost, you can have everything Jesus had as a man; and you can use all the things that the Spirit used through Jesus because you will be led by the Spirit all the time, not just part of the time.

The Bible tells us that Jesus was led by the Spirit to fast. **And Jesus being full of the Holy Ghost returned from Jordan, and was led by the Spirit into the wilderness, Being forty days tempted of the devil. And in those days he did eat nothing: and when they were ended, he afterward hungered** (Luke 4:1,2). We do not know how many times Jesus fasted; but we do know that on that first fast, He was led by the Spirit. After it was over, He met the devil head-on as recorded in Luke 4:3–13.

When you are full of the Holy Ghost, it is so simple for the Lord to lead you into a fast; but people do not always follow His lead because they are not full of the Holy Ghost. Some of you will finish a long fast and then pine away when you meet the devil head-on because you thought you would be at least halfway to Glory and that the devil would leave you alone for a while. Well, I have news for you: After a fast, the devil will come after you harder than ever to test what you have received. Did you get anything on the fast? Did you really fast through the blood? If so, then you have it made; and the devil will be put to flight. He will have to leave you for a season, but he will be back.

Jesus was full of the Holy Ghost; and after His fast, He returned in the power of the Spirit to Galilee. **And Jesus returned in the power of the Spirit into Galilee: and there went out a fame of him through all the region round about** (Luke 4:14). We must go to the world through the power of the Spirit, but you have to get ready to go; and you cannot do that unless you are yielded 100 percent to Him. We are facing something we have never faced before—all-out war between God and the devil, and we are right in the middle of it. We have to depend entirely on the Spirit; we will not make it any other way.

How much do you let the Spirit lead you? It doesn't mean you do not have the Holy Ghost because you fail to let Him lead you in everything. Some of you will make plans and conduct business without consulting the Holy Spirit until after you end up in trouble. Others of you will buy something and then wonder if you did the will of God, but that is a poor time to think about it. Why didn't you think about it before?—because you were not full of the Holy Ghost.

When you have the Holy Ghost but are not full of Him, you will use your own wisdom and knowledge; and the Lord will let you do that. Although you are not backslidden, you will still have to suffer because there is a price to pay for not remaining full of the Spirit. However, the Holy Spirit is very kind, and

He will not tell you that He is tired of fooling with you; instead, He picks up what pieces of your life He can and tries to make you whole again. If you furnish Him enough of yourself and remain in His hands long enough, He will put you back together.

YOU HAVE FREE CHOICE

When you are full of the Spirit, you will depend on the Lord for everything and let Him direct each one of your steps. The Bible says, **The steps of a good man are ordered by the LORD: and he delighteth in his way** (Psalm 37:23). Our steps are ordered by the Lord; but if you are not full of the Holy Ghost, you are not going to make all of those steps. How many times have you brought things upon yourself that have caused you to cry? Then the devil used those things to make you think that God did not love you as much as He loves others when the truth was that you just did not use the leadership of the Holy Spirit to help you make the steps that you should have made, and you made your own steps instead.

The Lord has given you the power to walk

right and to make the right decisions; but no matter what He gives you, you are still a free moral agent. You have free choice to decide how full you want to be of God. We sing this little chorus at my church:

Filled with God, filled with God,
Emptied of self, and filled with God.

How many people stay emptied of self? How many times in a day does self get in your way or hinder you from praying when the Spirit leads you to the prayer closet? It does not mean you are backslidden when you fail to pray at that time, but think how much better it will be if you do.

When the Spirit leads you to pray, be conscious of Him because He is right there with you to help you contact the Father. Some of you go into the prayer closet and act like you have to climb a ladder all the way up to Heaven to get to the throne of God, but that is not so. The Holy Spirit takes you right in before God; and no stairs, ladders or elevators are needed. He brings you in to worship the Lord in Spirit and in truth.

The Spirit knows the times when we need

to pray, and He knows when to wake us up to pray. The reason He never wakes some of you up to pray is because you don't get up. If the Lord wakes me up to pray, I don't lie there and think about it and then go back to sleep saying, "Lord, I know you called me sometime during the night; but you know my heart, and you know how tired I was." Yes, He knows our hearts; but then hear the Spirit say, "The Lord needed you to talk to Him, and He had laid everything aside for you to be with Him. He was going to use you as His holy instrument at that time to bring about a victory."

The Lord has made us so many promises about prayer, and God works through people with answered prayer. He can move on you to pray when a soul is about to drop into hell. It might be somebody in Africa, in China or in some other country; and you may be just the one who can pray the prayer that will keep that person from going to hell so the Lord can have time to work to get him or her saved. When you yield completely, the Holy Spirit uses you.

You must be led by the Spirit and by the

touch of the Lord and be so full of the Spirit that even sleep cannot destroy any of that fullness. You use it all for God and make that fullness available to the Lord at all times.

JUST LIKE JESUS

The Bible says, **For as he** [a man] **thinketh in his heart, so is he** (Proverbs 23:7). In other words, so is he with God and for God to work with. When you are full of the Spirit, **out of the abundance of the heart the mouth speaketh** (Matthew 12:34). The mouth must speak the abundance of love, grace, peace and joy; and that abundance is in your heart—the goodness of God, the truths of God and the greatness of God. It is wonderful for the mouth to speak from the abundance of the heart and for that abundance to be used by the Holy Spirit as He speaks to your mind. What is in your soul comes out through your lips and your vocal organ; so when you are full of the Holy Spirit, your words will not only edify and bless you, but they will also bless others. So think in your heart the thoughts of God—thoughts of victory, goodness and mercy.

The Lord wants us to have His thoughts.

Jesus as very man had the thoughts of the Father, and He longed for those thoughts. He was not only filled with the Holy Ghost, but He was full of the Holy Ghost; and He remained full at all times, so the Spirit was able to lead Him and use Him at any time in love in perfection.

You may say, "But He was the Son of God." Doesn't the Bible tell you that you are a son or a daughter of God through the blood? **The Spirit itself beareth witness with our spirit, that we are the children of God** (Romans 8:16). The Spirit will bear witness with your spirit, meaning your spirit matches the Holy Spirit. If they do not match, you are not saved. **And if children, then heirs; heirs of God, and joint-heirs with Christ; if so be that we suffer with him, that we may be also glorified together** (Romans 8:17). We are to take Jesus' place here on Earth.

Jesus made it plain to the disciples that as sons and daughters of God, they could have the same relationship with the Father that He had; and He let them hear His prayer to the Father for them. **I have manifested thy name**

unto the men which thou gavest me out of the world: thine they were, and thou gavest them me; and they have kept thy word... they are not of the world, even as I am not of the world. As thou hast sent me into the world, even so have I also sent them into the world. And for their sakes I sanctify myself, that they also might be sanctified through the truth. Neither pray I for these alone, but for them also which shall believe on me through their word; That they all may be one; as thou, Father, art in me, and I in thee, that they also may be one in us: that the world may believe that thou hast sent me. And the glory which thou gavest me I have given them; that they may be one, even as we are one: I in them, and thou in me, that they may be made perfect in one; and that the world may know that thou hast sent me, and hast loved them, as thou hast loved me (John 17:6,14,18–23). That is what the Holy Ghost can do for you through His keeping power.

No one else recorded that prayer but John, and he loved Jesus so much that he was right there listening to Jesus pray. Every child of God should be able to say, "I and my Father are one." The "I" comes first before "Father" because the Father is always ready for you to be one with Him, and Jesus is ready for you to be one, too.

THE SPIRIT HAS WHAT YOU NEED

If you do not stay full of God, other troubles, trials and persecutions will crowd in; but the Lord said, **Blessed are they which are persecuted for righteousness' sake: for theirs is the kingdom of heaven. Blessed are ye, when men shall revile you, and persecute you, and shall say all manner of evil against you falsely, for my sake. Rejoice, and be exceeding glad: for great is your reward in heaven: for so persecuted they the prophets which were before you** (Matthew 5:10–12). Instead of keeping your mind on your persecutions, think about this verse and let the joy of the Holy Ghost bubble over because you are pleasing God and your reward will be great. Then you will have joy instead of weakness, and you will have strength and power manifested through your life by the Holy Spirit. That power goes into action for you through wonderful thoughts.

You must keep your mind covered with the blood either by you using the blood on it or by letting the Spirit use the blood on it. Then the Holy Spirit flows divinity from your soul into your mind; and when you are full of the Holy Ghost, He flows everything you need at the moment you need it. If you are not full of the Holy Ghost, there is a delay. The Spirit has to wait, and there is a price to pay for making Him wait on you—you will not receive what you need at the time you need it.

Paul said, **But my God shall supply all your need according to his riches in glory by Christ Jesus** (Philippians 4:19). Many think, "The Lord must not love me because I see Him supply other people's needs, but He is never on time for me." The reason is that you are not full of the Spirit, and you are not on time with Him.

The problem is never that the Lord is not on time but that we are not on time with Him. When we are on time with God, He will work for us; and when we are full of the Holy Ghost, we will live in love in perfection and have the heart of God. It will beat for us if we let it, and it will give us everything we need each moment of the day.

God is so gracious that even when we were in sin, the Lord furnished us with air to breathe and blood to keep our bodies filled with life. He gifted us with sight and hearing; and even though we were sinners, He did not take those things away from us. So why do you let the enemy make you think that you cannot have all that Jesus brought, taught, used and put on display? You can accept it all and walk as Jesus walked if you are full of the Holy Ghost; but instead, you let disappointments take you over. Rather than going into the promises of God, you go into despair, doubt, fear and frustration. Then the Holy Spirit really has a struggle.

THE SPIRIT STRIVES FOR US

And the LORD said, My spirit shall not always strive with man (Genesis 6:3). Many people have never thought about the word "strive" and what God meant by that verse.

The word "strive" means "to contend," and the Spirit contends with us.

"Strive" also means "to make a great effort," but the Spirit will not always make a great effort toward man. There are already people for whom the Spirit is not making a great effort because they have disobeyed and said no to Him so many times. They will not live for God, so the Spirit is handicapped in their lives—He is crippled through such people and cannot make a great effort for them. He did make a great effort for them at one time just as He did in Noah's day when He strove with those wicked people and contended with them. The Holy Spirit made great efforts to save the human race, but the time came when the Spirit no longer put forth that effort because it was useless.

"Strive" also means "to try very hard," and the Spirit tries very hard with people at one time or another in their lives. With some, the Spirit has tried hard for years; but they will not yield.

Another definition for "strive" is "to be in conflict," and the Holy Spirit is at war with our human spirit. That human spirit of self stands up against God again and again, and the Holy Ghost battles with that spirit amidst great conflict.

"Strive" means "to struggle," and the Holy Spirit struggles with the self spirit just as Jacob struggled with the angel all the night through. **And Jacob was left alone; and there wrestled a man with him until the breaking of the day** (Genesis 32:24). If Jacob had been ready, yielded to the Spirit and full of the Holy Ghost, he would not have had to wrestle with the angel all night. The Lord never said we would have to do that; He said, **Ask, and it shall be given you; seek, and ye shall find; knock, and it shall be opened unto you** (Matthew 7:7).

And he [the angel] **said, Let me go, for the day breaketh. And he** [Jacob] **said, I will not let thee go, except thou bless me** (Genesis 32:26). If Jacob had been on blessing ground at that time, he would have been blessed because in the past, the Lord had blessed him every time Jacob had given Him the chance; but Jacob had a lot of deceit, disobedience and wrong ways in him, so the struggle was on.

It is amazing how we will contend with God and struggle with Him when we have a great need; however, the Spirit may have been struggling with us for years, but since we did not have a great need, we did not reach out for Him. That is why when America or other countries prosper, they forget God as a whole. If hard times would come and people were starving to death, they would be at the feet of the Lord. The churches would be filled, and people would be crying out to God for food. If it would stop raining for a year, there would be people who would get down to business with God. They would struggle with God instead of God having to struggle with them. They would contend with God crying, "Lord, we need this"; and they would make great efforts toward Him.

Many of God's own people are like that today. If they are not having any trouble, they do not give over to the Holy Spirit. They go on their way and miss church services to do other things. When their families come to visit, they think they have to be with them instead of going to church. What does the Holy Spirit say about that? Jesus said, **I must be about my Father's business** (Luke 2:49).

LET THE SPIRIT BE A WINNER

Yet another definition of "strive" is "to fight," as in striving against depression; and the Holy Spirit fights against oppression and depression. If He is not winning for you, it is because you will not make Him a winner. Jesus came to Earth and went all the way to Calvary to make us winners and to make God the Father, God the Son and God the Holy Ghost winners.

Some people look at God and think He is a God of defeat, but He is only defeated through man; and His Spirit will not always strive with man. He will not keep fighting losing battles; and one day, it will all be over. Man will no longer have free choice, and it will be total victory for God. Then in the Perfect Age, there will be victories for God through His holy people for 1000 years.

A final definition for "strive" is "to compete." You learned to compete with others when you were in grade school, whether it was in a ballgame or in other kinds of games. In the same way, the Holy Spirit strives or competes with that self of ours—sometimes He wins and sometimes He doesn't. That does not mean you are backslidden or that you do not have the Holy Ghost, but it does mean you are not full of Him. He has to compete against what you are doing; and because of that, you are in despair, full of fear or sick and afflicted, and those things are not your heritage.

The Bible says it is the will of the Lord for you to be in good health, and the Holy Spirit competes with you to win you over into good health. **Beloved, I wish above all things that thou mayest prosper and be in health, even as thy soul prospereth** (III John 1:2).

The Holy Spirit competes with you to win you over from depression into **joy unspeakable and full of glory** (I Peter 1:8). He competes with that self of yours to put you on believing ground so the doubt that you have will be defeated.

The Lord Jesus competed with the doubt that was in the heart of the man who brought his son to Jesus and said, **If thou canst do anything, have compassion on us, and help us** (Mark 9:22). The Lord immediately began to strive with him and said, **If thou canst believe, all things are possible to him that believeth** (Mark 9:23). Then the man yielded at once and **cried out, and said with tears, Lord, I believe; help thou mine unbelief** (Mark 9:24).

When we yield at once, the Lord can move at once; but when we know what He wants and we rebel against it, it may take us a little longer to come out. When that father said, *Lord, I believe; help thou mine unbelief,* the Lord had won. It was so very simple.

TAKE GOD'S WAY

When we look steadfastly to Heaven and are full of the Holy Ghost, the Lord can use any of us in an unbelievable way in this great hour. We are looking for Jesus to come, and we have no doubt that He is coming for those who are watching for Him. **Blessed are those servants, whom the lord when he cometh shall find watching: verily I say unto you, that he shall gird himself, and make them**

to sit down to meat, and will come forth and serve them (Luke 12:37). We must do more than watch for Him; we must be ready and helping to bring in the last part of the harvest because we are full of the Spirit, led by the Spirit and directed by the Spirit.

You must be led by the Spirit. Years ago, I had planned to build my ministry headquarters in the South; and I had never intended to become a pastor. I thought the Lord would let me be an evangelist for the rest of my life, but that was not the plan of God. He told me, "You are to go to Akron, Ohio and establish a work for me there." Then He said I would go to the nations. Thank God, He did not tell me how many years it would take, and the wonderful part was that I was led by the Spirit.

When the Lord told me to go to Akron, I dropped everything. I did not tell Him that I was planning to build my headquarters somewhere else, and I did not question Him about it. I thought I could build this work in a year and be ready to go to the nations. I did not know it would take more than fifty years to build it and to get ready for the outreach. The

Lord does not consider time; He counts on the obedience and love people have for Him. That is the way out of the problems, despair, doubt or trouble in your home.

CALLED OF GOD

When God called me to preach, He never mentioned finances or said He would supply my needs. He wanted me to preach His Gospel with no compromise just like Jesus had preached it when He walked among men. He wanted me to hold up the divine blood just like He holds it up and to make a born-again experience real to people just like Jesus had made it real to Nicodemus. He wanted me to be interested not just in crowds of people but in each individual.

In the past, the Lord has given His mind and His heart to one person, ten people or a multitude; and through much prayer and fasting, God has given His mind to me. Even among multitudes of people, God sees each person as an individual; and that is the way to get results on television, too. You cannot just imagine faceless people out there; you must know they are real individuals and that you are speaking to each one of them. That gives the Spirit a chance to draw each person to Calvary, to draw each one closer to God or into whatever God wants that person to do. Do you see how simple it is and why I put so much stress on the anointings and the fullness of the Spirit?

When the Lord called me to the healing ministry, I told Him to give it to other preachers and that I would never say anything against them. I believed in His gifts; but I knew that I would have to stay away from people so much of the time, and I love people. However, I was ready to obey Him in anything and even to die for His name's sake because I was full of the Holy Ghost.

There were thousands of hours of being shut away with the Lord and being taught demonology because there was much preparation to be made. I knew I would have no life of my own, and I am not looking for one. I am seeking to lose my life for Jesus and to give it all to Him. I am seeking to bring in every soul who can be brought in and to have His direction every moment that I have left. I am seeking ways and means that will enable us to reach more people because we do not have long, and the Spirit is desperate. He is striving with so many now, but He will not always do that.

The Lord is not striving with America as a whole in any great way today like He once did, but He is striving with Africa. People want to know why I go there; and the answer is because God is sending me, and the people are yielding to the Spirit of the Lord. The Holy Spirit has been striving with the people of Africa for years; but other spirits have bound so many of them—spirits of witchcraft, voodoo and all of the other darknesses of the devil. The Holy Spirit has struggled and contended with them and has sought day and night to lead them out, but how could they have been taught the right way if they did not have a teacher? The Lord has tried to raise up preachers, but they would not separate unto Him and would instead try to mix the devil's power with the power of God.

Down through the years, America has spent billions of dollars sending missionaries all around the world; but very few of them ever went to the nations with the signs and wonders of God, and even fewer went full of the Holy Ghost. For the Lord to do all the work He wants to in Africa or anywhere else, it has to be through the power of the Holy Ghost and the pure power of God. The Holy Ghost must be the one to shed abroad the love and faith of God in every person's heart who goes, or that person should stay home because that faith must be there to help the people.

PUT GOD FIRST

Some of you cannot stand to disappoint people in your family, and you will give over to them before you will give over to God. I have seen it happen again and again down through the years, and it is hard to tell how many hours the Spirit has been grieved because of it. When holidays or special events come, you think you have to be with your family even though they criticize your church, your salvation and your precious Holy Ghost. If you think you have to take all of that, then you are being deceived by the devil. The Lord said He came to separate families. **Think not that I am come to send peace on earth: I came not**

to send peace, but a sword. For I am come to set a man at variance against his father, and the daughter against her mother, and the daughter in law against her mother in law. And a man's foes shall be they of his own household (Matthew 10:34–36).

Jesus came with the sword of the Word, and the Word separates. You must not go to places where the Holy Ghost is mocked or not welcome. My family never did, and my mother was very bold about it; she would let people know in a hurry what she believed. Our relatives knew what she believed; and later, it brought many of them to God, and they are in Heaven today.

God says we can have no other gods before Him. **For thou shalt worship no other god: for the LORD, whose name is Jealous, is a jealous God** (Exodus 34:14). Nevertheless, we will make our own little gods if we are not careful, and those little things can draw you away from the path the Lord wants you on. On God's path, you may have been almost to victory; but you went to the left or the right when you should have gone straight ahead. If you had been full of the Spirit, there would have been no room for whatever took your attention and your steadfast look off of Jesus.

When you separate from those whom you need to stay away from, you will never walk alone because God walks with those who separate themselves unto Him; and He will always hold your hand. He sent the great Comforter to live within, and nobody can steal Him away from you. Nobody can entice Him to leave you, and nobody can turn Him against you.

There is so much God wants you to know in this final hour. God needs every one of us; and the Lord does not only want us to be filled with the Holy Ghost, He wants us to be full of the Holy Ghost so that we will be just like His Son, Jesus. Just think what we can accomplish if everybody will follow the paths God wants us to every day. He can feed us the thoughts of strength and greatness He wants us to have. He can speak through us and anoint us and make prayer such a reality that we know we are talking to Him in a direct way. We will be led of the Spirit to fast, and there is nothing like being led of the Spirit.

CHAPTER 8

The Fullness of the Spirit Brings Reality

When you have the reality of being full of the Spirit, you will have the reality of Calvary; and you must have that reality and keep the sufferings of Calvary ever before you. Christ's suffering must become real to you or you will not sacrifice all you should or walk and act just like Jesus did. Jesus taught us to talk to the Father and say, **Father, if it be possible, let this cup pass from me: nevertheless not as I will, but as thou wilt** (Matthew 26:39). You will always have that last part in your spirit when you are full of the Holy Ghost.

When you have the reality of Jesus' sufferings, you will have the reality of the power of His resurrection. Paul said, **That I may know him, and the power of his resurrection, and the fellowship of his sufferings, being made conformable unto his death** (Philippians 3:10). Many of you do not really want to know Jesus in His sufferings because in order to know Him that way, you will have to suffer for His name's sake. **If we suffer, we shall also reign with him** (II Timothy 2:12).

If you are not full of the Holy Ghost, He cannot keep the reality of Christ's sufferings and the power of His resurrection ever before you. You will make room for other things, and you have the privilege of doing that. As long as you do not grieve the Spirit over and over, quench His Spirit willfully or resist Him, He will stay; but He is always seeking for everyone to be full of the Holy Ghost in this final hour.

When you are full of the Holy Ghost, you will accept the whole truth and all the ways of Jesus. You will trace and retrace His steps in the New Testament when He walked upon

Earth as a man. Being full of the Holy Ghost brings the reality of God, and He is there to anoint you so you can pray. He will never leave you alone in your prayer chamber; He is always with you to help you get your prayers through.

When you are full of the Holy Ghost, you are conscious of Him living and dwelling in you. If you have Him but are not full of Him, divine love and joy will not flow all the time; and you will let depression and despair take over. Despair will come even to those who are full of the Holy Ghost; but they will be conscious that it has come, and they will know how to get rid of it. Feelings may come for the moment, but you must go beyond feelings and brush them aside knowing that **the just shall live by faith** (Hebrews 10:38).

YIELD TO GOD'S WILL

When you are full of the Holy Ghost, you have the reality that God's grace is sufficient. Paul asked the Lord three times to take away a devil who was stirring up trouble everywhere he went. **There was given to me a thorn in the flesh, the messenger of Satan**

to buffet me, lest I should be exalted above measure. For this thing I besought the Lord thrice, that it might depart from me (II Corinthians 12:7,8).

Paul had so much faith in God that he did not beg Him; he just kept asking, and that was an act of faith. When you start begging God, you are doubting. Jesus said to ask; and when you do, you are using faith. You can ask the Lord for something more than one time as long as He has not already told you something different from what you are wanting, but do not beg Him!

Some of you do not get much out of prayer because you think you have to pray in a particular way that you have been taught to pray in the past; but the result is that you just talk, talk, talk. When you get tired of talking, you stop, sigh and leave your prayer closet; but that is not the way to do it.

Paul knew the Lord always heard him; so even though God had not answered him, he did not beg. He just kept asking in humility, in the spirit of wanting to do the whole will of God and in being yielded to the Holy Ghost

100 percent. Paul had patience like Jesus did—he was very longsuffering, and he proved it when he did not get impatient with God. It is easy to become impatient with God, but it is a dangerous thing to do.

Paul was expecting an answer from God; and the third time Paul asked, he got his answer. **And he** [the Lord] **said unto me, My grace is sufficient for thee: for my strength is made perfect in weakness. Most gladly therefore will I rather glory in my infirmities, that the power of Christ may rest upon me** (II Corinthians 12:9). Without this answer, Paul probably would have asked a fourth or even a fifth time because he was really being hindered. He believed it would be better for that devil to stop following him everywhere he went and stirring up the people because he could get more done; but the Lord's answer was, *My grace is sufficient for thee: for my strength is made perfect in weakness.*

You will always keep your eyes on grace when you are full of the Holy Ghost. Paul knew that his strength was weak and that the perfect love, perfect power, perfect greatness, perfect hand and perfect will of God were showing through the strength he was receiving. His strength was coming from On High, and he knew he would have enough of it to overcome anything.

We too can have that spiritual power, that wonderful presence of the Holy Ghost living on the inside of us. He dwells in that presence, and it is ours to use. It is Heaven here on Earth, and it makes an Eden on the inside of us. Praise God! Dwelling in that presence is as close as you will get to Heaven here on Earth, so you must get it and enjoy it until you get there.

Having the reality of the will of the Lord cannot be a part-time thing; you must want the whole will of God all the time. However, when you are not full of the Holy Ghost, He is not able to guide you all the time. You have free choice to do things that are not necessarily sinful and to walk paths that do not necessarily mean you are backslidden, but they are not things the Holy Spirit would do or the paths He would guide you on. When you follow your own paths, the Spirit cannot do everything with you that He was able to do with Jesus when He was a man.

Jesus taught the disciples to pray, **Our Father which art in heaven, Hallowed be thy name. Thy kingdom come. Thy will be done in earth, as it is in heaven** (Matthew 6:9,10). "Thy will" is God's perfect will, and nothing less will do than for the will of the Lord to be done in you and through you here on Earth. The whole will of God will not be done here on Earth until the Perfect Age; and at that time, those who do not want to do it will be forced into it. But now, you can have God's will in your heart if you want it; and it will be just like it will be in Heaven. Up there, you will not be looking for any more of the perfect will of God than you are looking for right here on Earth; but that can only happen when you are full of the Holy Ghost.

WIN THE LOST

When you are full of the Holy Ghost, you always have the reality of soul winning; and souls will ever be before you. Jesus said to His disciples, **The harvest truly is plenteous, but the labourers are few** (Matthew 9:37).

Souls are ready to be won; but if you do not always keep the harvest fields before you, you will not see that they are ripe or feel the urgency of being a reaper. You will think you have more time than you really do, and you will take more time doing other things than you should. This does not mean that you are backslidden, but it does mean that you are not full of the Holy Ghost.

Pray ye therefore the Lord of the harvest, that he will send forth labourers into his harvest (Matthew 9:38). Jesus said this when He was teaching the disciples about the Holy Spirit, and many people do not realize that the Holy Spirit is the Lord of the harvest. The field is His, and He has been ordained by God to reap the harvest through people.

When we have the Lord of the harvest directing us, He will see to it that we have everything we need; but we have to accept it. We have to see Him as the Lord of the harvest and know that He is Lord of all when we go to the mission field. We must leave here with that reality in our lives, and then we must be filled with the Spirit and have the

Holy Ghost working within us. We must be vessels who are consecrated and dedicated for the Master's use.

Jesus said He would *send forth labourers into His harvest,* and He will send them forth! We must be sent of God to bring in the real harvest, and that is why we win so many thousands in our overseas crusades.

God is now sending me to Africa; He gave me a burden for the African people many years ago. As a child, I would listen with complete attention whenever missionaries from Africa would come to our church. When they would mention Africa, they had my attention. I could never get enough of the things the missionaries shared about their experiences in Africa, and I did not know that the Lord was preparing me to go there one day. The Lord of the harvest was getting me ready to bring in a great harvest; and now, He is raising up many partners in this Jesus ministry to help me do it. They are a part of this great work, and the Lord has sent me to be used by Him to gather more laborers. God has indeed put together a mighty army, and we must not let anything stop us. You who are planning to be one of the laborers for the Lord of the harvest must pray and seek God like never before so you will be able to consecrate and dedicate yourselves like never before.

The Bible says, **Go ye into all the world, and preach the gospel to every creature** (Mark 16:15). We have the reality of the Great Commission just like the apostles had when they went forth and evangelized the known world in thirty-three years. Thank God we have faster means today because there are over six billion people on Earth now; and the Lord is making it possible for us to reach them through radio, television, the Internet and the printed page. Our website is going all over the world with Gospel messages, miracles and singing; and people are sending in their email messages to let us know they are watching.

YOU MUST BE CONSECRATED

To be full of the Holy Ghost means you are holy, set apart and consecrated to Him. Caleb, one of the twelve spies of the Children of Israel, told Moses that he had wholly followed the Lord; and Moses promised him a mountain. Later, Caleb told Joshua, **I wholly followed the LORD my God. And Moses sware on that day, saying, Surely the land whereon thy feet have trodden shall be thine inheritance, and thy children's forever, because thou hast wholly followed the LORD my God** (Joshua 14:8,9).

God did not deny Caleb's request; and five years later, Caleb received that mountain. **Now therefore give me this mountain, whereof the LORD spake in that day... And Joshua blessed him, and gave unto Caleb the son of Jephunneh Hebron for an inheritance** (Joshua 14:12,13). Caleb had asked for something big that would bless his family, and we can ask God for big things, too, if we are not being selfish about it.

When you are wholly consecrated to God and full of the Holy Ghost, the Lord can use you all the time. The Lord needs people He can use in this final hour, and this is a great truth you must remember: You must consecrate and give yourself to the Lord so completely that He can use you 100 percent. He needs you to be holy and ready to do whatever

He wants. Every true Christian worker should be set apart and consecrated to the Lord.

Don't look at other people and gauge your life by them when you have the true and perfect example—Jesus Christ. He took on a body of flesh just like we have and a flesh mind like ours. The Holy Ghost cannot be your example because He did not come down here as a man; He came as a divine person in the Trinity of the Godhead.

BE AN OVERSEER OF YOURSELF

The Bible says, **Take heed therefore unto yourselves, and to all the flock, over the which the Holy Ghost hath made you overseers** (Acts 20:28). The Holy Ghost has ordained every person to be an overseer of himself, yet some people do not realize this. The devil cannot keep us from having the greatness of God, but self can.

Self is your worst enemy, not the devil; but it is hard to look into the mirror and say, "There is enemy number one in my life." We would rather see a picture of a gangster on a "wanted" poster with a caption that says, "Public Enemy Number One."

You have to get self out of the way or you will be like a cloud without rain. **Whoso boasteth himself of a false gift is like clouds and wind without rain** (Proverbs 25:14). Clouds will not help us if there is no rain in them; and if we do not have the rain of the Holy Spirit in our spirits and attempt to serve without Him, we will be clouds without rain in this final hour. We will not be seasoned to bring in the harvest throughout the world.

When you bear fruit, that is the ordination that will glorify God. **Ye have not chosen me, but I have chosen you, and ordained you, that ye should go and bring forth fruit, and that your fruit should remain: that whatsoever ye shall ask of the Father in my name, he may give it you** (John 15:16). Those were powerful words that Jesus spoke to the disciples when He was here, and He is still saying them to people today; but you cannot use the name of Jesus like you should without the Holy Ghost.

Some people miss it because they think that when you take on the new man, you do not have to look out for the new self. The truth is that you have to look out for the new self even more in order to keep that new self in the righteousness and holiness of God. Paul said, **And that ye put on the new man, which after God is created in righteousness and true holiness** (Ephesians 4:24). The Lord is letting you know that you must take heed to yourself—the new self, not the old self.

WHAT IS AN OVERSEER?

To be an "overseer" means "to watch over or manage," so you have to manage your new self. That is easy to do when you are full of the Holy Ghost; but when you are not full of Him, it will be much harder for you to do that. When self gets out of control and causes you to lose your temper and act in ways you should not act, you are not being a good overseer.

To "oversee" means "to supervise," and you have to supervise and watch over self more than you do anybody else. Do not try to supervise others until you have first supervised your own self.

To "oversee" means "to examine and inspect," and the Holy Spirit will help you to do that without even charging you. The

Bible says, **Let a man examine himself** (I Corinthians 11:28). This is talking about a person with the new mind; so first, you must examine yourself to see if you have a new mind, to see if you are in the faith and full of faith. **Examine yourselves, whether ye be in the faith** (II Corinthians 13:5). If you are in the faith, then you are in the truth; so examine yourself to see if you have made any room for doubt. Doubts will come; but if you are full of the Holy Ghost, they cannot stay.

In divine visitations, the Lord told me of this great hour. He spent so much time with me that I lost count of the days because I was in the very presence of God. In one visitation, I actually walked with Him. I did not see all of Him; but as we walked together, I could see His leg by my side, and my head was about even with His kneecap. That was the only time God ever came down to walk with me in a form that I could actually see, and I never even thought to look up into His face.

During that vision, God showed me the greatness of this hour and the unbelievable things to come; and as I watched and beheld,

I never doubted one thing. It was so fantastic that when I began to tell other fellow ministers about it, they thought I had gone crazy; but I knew it was all real. I also knew that if it was not real, there was no need for me ever to open the Bible again. I was so sure of it that I could have walked out and staked my life on every bit of it.

LET YOUR MIND BE RENEWED

The Bible tells you about your mind; and in Ephesians it says, **Be renewed in the spirit of your mind** (Ephesians 4:23). Many people do not take care of their mind even though they have been made an overseer of it. What does the word "renew" mean to you? It means "to make new again," and you renew your mind by giving it over to the Holy Spirit; He makes it like new. No matter how many battles you are having or how much trouble you have already gone through, the Spirit makes your mind brand new, crystal clear and fresh as the morning dew.

"Renew" also means "to make young," so you do not have to worry about getting too old to think right. Let the Lord renew your mind daily; and He will make it like a young one, as fresh as if you were starting again in your youth. If some of you did not take care of your bodies any more than you do your minds, it would be bad.

"Renew" means "to give new spiritual strength to." Your mind has to have that strength, and the Holy Ghost is there to work through your mind. Remember that your mind is not sealed with divine blood, so you have to depend on the Holy Spirit and yourself to look after it.

The mind moves so fast that it can quickly get over into the wrong territories, so you have to survey it and find out if it is still where it ought to be—home with the Holy Spirit. If you have the Holy Spirit abiding in you, you must not let your mind wander away. You have to survey it and find out if everything is in order. Are you in possession of your mind or just your soul? The devil will worry some of you to death through your mind, so you need to examine and inspect your mind daily. You can have all you need for your mind every day when you are full of the Spirit.

When you are born again, you take on a mind that has been re-created in righteousness and true holiness. It is the same perfect mind that God gave Adam and Eve, but even they had to be overseers of their minds. **And the LORD God commanded the man, saying, Of every tree of the garden thou mayest freely eat: But of the tree of the knowledge of good and evil, thou shalt not eat of it: for in the day that thou eatest thereof thou shalt surely die** (Genesis 2:16,17). Adam and Eve were to have guarded their minds and never gone to that death tree. Adam guarded his mind, but Eve did not guard hers. Adam was an overseer of his mind; he supervised it and took orders from God only. Eve, however, did not look out for her mind; and she yielded to serpent-talk.

If you are not the overseer of your mind in righteousness and holiness, you will listen to serpent-talk; and it will hinder you, depress you and cause you despair. The Holy Ghost will never give those things to you who are full of the Spirit. Now, it does not mean that you are backslidden when you do have those things, but it does mean that you are not overseeing your mind the way the Lord said you must. I say again that God has ordained you as the overseer of your own mind, and the Holy Ghost gives you the strength to do that. He makes the mind better in the Spirit so it can easily receive what He, the guiding Spirit, says.

Another definition of "renew" is "to replace with something new or of the same kind." When the Spirit renews your mind, He can replace it with something brand new if you need Him to; or He can replace it with more of what you had—things you are no longer using or have lost. If you have not sinned against God, He will replace what was in your mind or put in a fresh supply. How often do you let the Holy Spirit put a fresh supply in your mind? You may tell people, "I am so troubled and worried, and I don't know what to do." Well, I am telling you what to do, so stop telling people that you don't know. You know what to do, but whether you do it or not is up to you.

"Renew" means "to become new again,

to begin again or to start over." Don't get disgusted with your mind; just get it renewed. How often will you have to do that? You are the overseer, so you must decide what your mind needs. The Bible says, **And walk in love, as Christ also hath loved us, and hath given himself for us an offering and a sacrifice to God for a sweet-smelling savour** (Ephesians 5:2). That is the kind of mind you need.

INSTRUCTIONS FROM EPHESIANS

Let no man deceive you with vain words: for because of these things cometh the wrath of God upon the children of disobedience (Ephesians 5:6). When you have a mind that will not let people deceive you, you will prove what is the acceptable will of God. **Proving what is acceptable unto the Lord** (Ephesians 5:10).

Paul went on to say, **And have no fellowship with the unfruitful works of darkness, but rather reprove them** (Ephesians 5:11). You cannot have any fellowship with the unfruitful works of darkness in the world. You cannot hang around people who have the spirit of the devil, and you do not have to.

If they are around you or live in your house, then pray the roof down on them. You have a mind that can do it when your mind is right and works with the Holy Spirit 100 percent.

Wherefore be ye not unwise, but understanding what the will of the Lord is (Ephesians 5:17). Do you have complete understanding of what the will of God is for you? So many people struggle to find God's will when the thing to do is just to stay full of the Holy Ghost; then you will have that will. This is what I have done, and it works.

When I was saved, I really lived with God. I was not just filled with the Holy Ghost; I was full of the Holy Ghost, and that was why the Lord was able to start preaching through me within just five or six weeks. People said I preached just like a seasoned preacher, but the Lord was the one who was giving the messages to me because I was full of the Holy Ghost.

Ephesians gives us the pattern for the Spirit-filled life. **And be not drunk with wine, wherein is excess; but be filled with the Spirit** (Ephesians 5:18). When you are filled with the Spirit and full of the Spirit, you will be **speaking to yourselves in psalms and hymns and spiritual songs** (Ephesians 5:19). I stopped listening to all of the world's music when I found the Lord, and I had loved it. The world's music gets into your bones, and it begins to move you. I loved the jitterbug dance, and I loved waltzing. I thought it was great to be able to glide a girl across the dance floor, but all of that left me. I spoke to myself the things of God in psalms, hymns and spiritual songs. That was all I wanted, and I did not feed myself anything else.

Singing and making melody in your heart to the Lord (Ephesians 5:19). When you do that, the Holy Ghost has 100 percent right of way in your life; and you will be **giving thanks always for all things unto God and the Father in the name of our Lord Jesus Christ** (Ephesians 5:20).

Ephesians goes on to tell you that you can have the whole armor of God that we studied earlier. **Put on the whole armour of God, that ye may be able to stand against the wiles of the devil. For we wrestle not**

against flesh and blood, but against principalities, against powers, against the rulers of the darkness of this world, against spiritual wickedness in high places (Ephesians 6:11,12). You can have the Holy Ghost and not have on the whole armor of God; but when you are full of the Holy Ghost, you will have it all.

FORGET YOURSELF

The disciples who were full of the Holy Ghost did not go out to minister until they were sent. **So they, being sent forth by the Holy Ghost, departed** (Acts 13:4). Paul made three great missionary journeys, and he was directed by the Spirit every time. It is wonderful to be directed by the Holy Spirit, and you can have the mind for it. The question should not be, "How can I get a hold of and use the Spirit?" It should be, "How can the Holy Spirit get a hold of and use me?" This is what being full of the Holy Ghost is all about.

I heard one preacher say, "Oh, if I could just forget myself." What a thing for a preacher to say, but some of them need to say it. That preacher would forget about himself if he was more taken up with Christ, and he would be more taken up with Christ if he were more fully in the hands of the Holy Ghost and full of the Spirit.

For **where the Spirit of the Lord is, there is liberty** (II Corinthians 3:17). This means that there is liberty where the Holy Spirit is Lord; and if He is Lord of your life, He has liberty. If He is not Lord of your life, you may have the Holy Ghost dwelling in you; but you are not full of the Holy Ghost or enjoying the liberties that you should be. You have gotten yourself into bondages that are not willful sins, but they are hindering you.

As children of God, we are to have all the liberty of Christ; so what you need to do is turn against yourself. It may be easy for you to pout at other people, but have you ever pouted at yourself? It may be easy to open your mouth and spew out garbage on somebody else, but have you ever done that to yourself and really told self off? The first qualification of following Jesus is to deny self. **Then said Jesus unto his disciples, If any man will come after me, let him deny**

himself, and take up his cross, and follow me (Matthew 16:24).

You have to turn against and deny self; and when you keep self down, you will keep Christ up. However, if you keep self up, you will keep Christ down; and He cannot do for you what He planned to. This is why it is great when you put off the old self and put on the new.

KEEP YOUR EYES ON JESUS

Nothing can separate us from the love of God, and Paul proved it. He said, **For I am persuaded, that neither death, nor life, nor angels, nor principalities, nor powers, nor things present, nor things to come, Nor height, nor depth, nor any other creature, shall be able to separate us from the love of God, which is in Christ Jesus our Lord** (Romans 8:38,39).

Paul remained persuaded because he was full of the Holy Ghost; and when you are full of the Holy Ghost, you will stay persuaded, too. When you are not full of the Holy Ghost, you may think at times that nothing can separate you; but when opposition comes in like a storm and covers you up like the waters covered the Earth in Noah's day, you are likely to summon your own forces to help you. Either that or you will just throw up your hands in despair and say, "What is the use? I am not getting anywhere!" When you are full of the Holy Ghost, you will not do that no matter how much trouble comes your way. What you should do is trust in the Lord; but to do that, you must be full of the Holy Ghost all the time.

How do you trust in the Lord?—by keeping your eyes on the overcoming Christ. You must spend all the time you can with Jesus; He is the best company you will ever find. After I was saved, I did not miss any of my so-called friends of the world. I did not hang around with them or go anywhere with them. My brother and I had been buddies and had run around together, but I stopped doing that at once. I had been taught that when you became saved, you were to leave the world behind and quit all your sinning; you were not to take any of it with you.

You cannot look at anybody but Jesus; and the Holy Spirit will help you to stay focused and to keep your mind on Jesus…if you want to keep it there. However, since you are ordained the overseer over your mind, the Holy Ghost can only work with you as you work to do what the Word has said you should.

The Holy Spirit works only with the Word, never outside of it. Every one of His works and every move He makes are in harmony with the Word. He directs you and gives you the energy and the power to keep moving on, and you will get great results.

Paul told Timothy, **For God hath not given us the spirit of fear; but of power, and of love, and of a sound mind** (II Timothy 1:7). That is God's promise to you, but a sound mind depends on how you take care of your mind so the Holy Spirit can use it all the time. Then He can see perfectly through your eyes, hear in perfection through your spiritual ears and speak through you at any time...and He does talk. You will also have the Spirit of power to use; and it will go forth in your voice, in your eyes and from your body.

The Holy Spirit of truth does not leave you with any clouds of doubt. Doubt and unbelief only come from that which is false, and there is nothing false about the Holy Spirit. There are no spirits of doubt or fear in the Spirit of truth, only godly fear which means to honor God. **The fear of the LORD is the beginning of wisdom** (Psalm 111:10).

Two of the gifts of the Spirit are wisdom and knowledge, so why not let the Holy Spirit give you wisdom and knowledge for things? **If any of you lack wisdom, let him ask of God, that giveth to all men liberally, and upbraideth not; and it shall be given him** (James 1:5).

The Holy Spirit uses God's ultimate anointings, and the Lord is now pouring them out; but the Spirit can only use those anointings through you by your yielding to Him. **The yoke shall be destroyed because of the anointing** (Isaiah 10:27), and the anointing is power. Yield to truth and let the Spirit direct you and take you to where He wants you to be. He knows where He can use those divine, supernatural anointings, and He works those anointings through you; but He can only use what is in your soul, so they must be in there for Him to use them. In the same way, divine faith and love have to be in your soul for the Spirit to be able to use them.

THE FULLNESS BRINGS DELIVERANCE

When you are completely full of the Holy Ghost all the time, the nine fruits of the Spirit are produced in abundance because your heart is full of His presence; and the fruit you bear comes forth from the indwelling of the presence of the Holy Spirit. Then the keeping of that presence brings forth the nine fruits of the Spirit in full abundance—perfect fruit from Heaven.

With all of this on the inside of you, it is the closest you will get to Heaven without actually being there. We did not get into the first Eden; but we can be in the second Eden, not by having Earth's fruit but by having Heaven's fruit. Ponder the indwelling of the Spirit's presence—He will dwell with you and shall be in you.

If you are full of the Holy Ghost, angels will be real to you just as they were to Peter. He thought at first that he was having a dream, but then he accepted it as reality because he was full of the Holy Ghost. **Peter therefore**

was kept in prison: but prayer was made without ceasing of the church unto God for him. And when Herod would have brought him forth, the same night Peter was sleeping between two soldiers, bound with two chains: and the keepers before the door kept the prison. And, behold, the angel of the Lord came upon him, and a light shined in the prison: and he smote Peter on the side, and raised him up, saying, Arise up quickly. And his chains fell off from his hands. And the angel said unto him, Gird thyself, and bind on thy sandals. And so he did. And he saith unto him, Cast thy garment about thee, and follow me. And he went out, and followed him; and wist not that it was true which was done by the angel; but thought he saw a vision. When they were past the first and the second ward, they came unto the iron gate that leadeth unto the city; which opened to them of his own accord: and they went out, and passed on through one street; and forthwith the angel departed from him. And when Peter was come to himself, he said, Now I

know of a surety, that the Lord hath sent his angel, and hath delivered me out of the hand of Herod, and from all the expectation of the people of the Jews (Acts 12:5–11).

Herod was going to kill Peter the next day; but still, he was asleep between the guards. That shows that he was full of the Holy Ghost, and he had no room for any doubt or fear to linger. Peter had a mind that was being renewed daily by the Spirit Himself, a mind like Christ had when He walked among men.

My soul cries out, and the Spirit cries out through me for the Lord's people to hurry and come on into this greatness. Don't wait for anybody else—husband, wife, children, brothers, sisters, mothers or daddies. Come on in now!

BATTLES OF THE MIND

The battles of the mind are not yours to keep or to be tormented with. They are the strategy of the devil, and the Lord told me what his strategy would be in this final hour. Over thirty-five years ago, He gave me His first message on the battles of the mind; and I had never before heard anybody preach on them, and they were never mentioned in my theological school. The Lord laid them out to me and said they would be the fieriest trials for God's people in the last hour.

Many of you are now having those fiery trials, and it is as if some strange thing has happened to you. You feel so strange that you wonder if you have backslidden, but the Bible said it would be that way. **Beloved, think it not strange concerning the fiery trial which is to try you, as though some strange thing happened unto you** (I Peter 4:12).

The Lord told me that He gets no glory out of the battles of the mind. You have to give those battles to the Holy Spirit through faith and truth, and He will take them if you have Him living in you; but He must become living reality to you for you to overcome all those battles like you should. You have to learn to turn your mind battles over to the Holy Spirit just like you would unload something you are carrying. If I were to tell you that I would take all of your mind battles, most of you would unload them in a hurry; but I am not the cure. The Holy Spirit is the one who will take those battles if you will just say, "Holy Spirit, here they are."

When you give something to somebody to carry, you do not continue to carry it yourself; but that is what some of you do with the battles of the mind. You go on being tormented, cast down and defeated when you could be gathering more and more strength from On High.

Jesus gave His life for lost humanity, and winning those souls is the burden we are to carry. When you do that, the Holy Spirit will take care of so much for you without you even asking Him. When you carry that burden and really tarry for souls, He will do things that you may have had to pray and pray for; but you will not even have to pray for them. *The more you give your life, your heart and your soul to the great commission of Jesus, the more your cares in life will be taken care of by the Holy Spirit Himself. That is thus saith the Lord;* so think on that, and it will be a great help and blessing to you.

THE WILL IS IN THE WORD

The Lord is revealing all of His will in this final hour. He is revealing everything about

His Word and every passage of scripture He possibly can. The Bible is an Earth book, not a Heaven book; and we need to use it now. It describes everything we need and lays out all the paths for us and the whole will of God from here to Heaven. It lays out God's plan for the Rapture to take place and tells us the signs to look for, and He is giving us those signs. He said that those who walk in the light will know the season. **I am the light of the world: he that followeth me shall not walk in darkness, but shall have the light of life** (John 8:12). You will not know the exact hour; but if you are full of the Lord, you will know that this is the season.

You need to get into the teachings of Christ through John. John told us more about Jesus and the Holy Ghost than anyone else; and remember, the Bible tells us that John was the disciple whom Jesus loved. He stayed close to Jesus, and he learned much because you learn by being with Jesus. I did not learn the things I am teaching you by being with other people; I learned them by being with Jesus and through the Holy Spirit teaching me. He teaches me different lessons and lets me know about Himself; and He takes me to the Word of God because the Word—the truth—must back up everything I teach.

CHAPTER 9

The Disciples Won When They Were Full of the Holy Ghost

Are you filled with the Holy Spirit or full of the Holy Spirit—which is it? You can go beyond and be full of the Spirit just as some of the disciples in the Early Church did. Unfortunately, they did not all go beyond to be full of the Holy Ghost; but the Lord gave to all those who yielded everything and desired much from Him.

And the disciples were filled with joy, and with the Holy Ghost (Acts 13:52). These things did not come until many days after the Holy Ghost had fallen, but at last the disciples became full of joy because they were not just filled but full of the Holy Ghost. You can be full of joy, too. I bubble over with it; but although some of you have joy, you will not let it run over. The Bible says, **Ask, and ye shall receive, that your joy may be full** (John 16:24); and "full" means complete. It takes the Holy Ghost to keep you happy.

When you are filled with joy, you will also be full of peace and strength. **The joy of the LORD is your strength** (Nehemiah 8:10). The inner person, the real you, needs a lot of strength; and divine peace, joy, gentleness, goodness and faith all go along with the fullness of the Spirit.

Then we are **strengthened with might by his Spirit in the inner man** (Ephesians 3:16). The power of the Spirit is sufficient for the inner person, and He can give you all the strength you need to climb every hill and to come out of every valley.

Jesus was tired from His journey when He met the woman at the well. The disciples had gone to buy food; and when they returned, they could not understand why Jesus was talking to a Samaritan woman when normally, the Jews had nothing to do with the Samaritans. The disciples were starving and wanted to start eating, and they wanted to give Jesus food, too; **But he said unto them, I have meat to eat that ye know not of** (John 4:32). When you are full of the Holy Ghost, you have meat from Heaven to eat that the world does not know about. You have peace and happiness that the world does not understand.

The Holy Ghost strengthens and renews only the new, inner man, not the old man—the Spirit does not want him to be strengthened. Then He uses that new man to glorify Jesus and the Father.

PRAY FOR HOLY BOLDNESS

At first, the disciples were not full of boldness; but when they were persecuted, punished and thrown in jail, they gathered together and prayed for holy boldness—they knew they had to have it. I am sure they did not know that taking Jesus' place would call for more and more persecutions. **And now, Lord, behold their threatenings: and grant unto thy servants, that with all boldness they may speak thy word, By stretching forth thine**

hand to heal; and that signs and wonders may be done by the name of thy holy child Jesus. And when they had prayed, the place was shaken where they were assembled together; and they were all filled with the Holy Ghost, and they spake the word of God with boldness (Acts 4:29–31).

When the holy boldness came, the Lord shook the place where they were assembled; and the Bible says they were all filled with the Holy Ghost. The Bible already says in Acts 2:4 that the disciples had received the Holy Ghost, so I sought the Lord for what He meant by Acts 4:31. Then I came into the light of what the Lord meant—those disciples had not only been filled with the Spirit; they were full of Him. They had not taken on other things of the world around them, and they had not put family ahead of the Lord. They had put the Lord first in everything and had obeyed Him. Before they would obey self, friends or family, they obeyed the voice of the Lord and followed the leadership of the Holy Spirit.

Later, the Bible says, **Long time therefore abode they speaking boldly in the Lord,**

which gave testimony unto the word of his grace, and granted signs and wonders to be done by their hands (Acts 14:3). Notice that all of this gave testimony to the Word of His grace. The disciples had God's holy hands; they were full of the Holy Ghost, and they were full of boldness. The Lord had granted them the grace for signs and wonders to be done by their hands.

God is going to use His true children in this final hour to stretch forth their hands to the lost with signs and wonders, and people throughout the whole Earth must see these signs and wonders. Those who want to win souls at home and abroad must seek God with their whole hearts and be so dedicated and consecrated to Him that He can use their hands as His very own—this is what the Lord is looking for. He told us to lift up holy hands, and the Lord can only use holy hands. **I will therefore that men pray everywhere, lifting up holy hands, without wrath and doubting** (I Timothy 2:8). Only those with a clean tongue can lift up holy hands; so if your tongue is not clean, your hands are not clean. If your spirit is not clean, your tongue is not pure.

SERVE THE LORD

And in those days, when the number of the disciples was multiplied, there arose a murmuring of the Grecians against the Hebrews, because their widows were neglected in the daily ministration. Then the twelve called the multitude of the disciples unto them, and said, It is not reason that we should leave the word of God, and serve tables. Wherefore, brethren, look ye out among you seven men of honest report, full of the Holy Ghost and wisdom, whom we may appoint over this business (Acts 6:1–3).

The disciples were having a problem because the Grecians who had come into salvation were complaining that their widows were not being taken care of. But it was wonderful that the disciples were full of the Holy Ghost and full of the wisdom, the knowledge, the greatness and the thoughts of God; and Peter and the others said, "We cannot stop ministering the Word because it is paramount. Choose seven men who are of honest report and full of the Holy Ghost to take care of this."

The widows' husbands were gone, and they were suffering; so the men who were chosen had to be of honest report. Why?—because they would be raising finances to take care of the widows, and they had to be able to be trusted with that money. They also had to have the wisdom to know how to take care of those who were in need, how to rightly divide the money and how to look after them with the tenderness of the Lord. The widows needed to be served God's love, not just food and clothing.

The Lord is ready to give us great love today, but you have to use His love. He gave me greater love than I had ever found in Him after He had taken Angel home. He flooded me with more love than I could use day after day. When I would go home, every room, every nook and every corner of my house would be filled with Him. Sometimes in my great sorrow and because I am just human, I would sink down and start sobbing my heart out. At those times, I could not use the love

God had there for me; but when I would finish crying, I would turn to His love and start using it. Then I would cry, "Oh, Lord, I just have to be loved; I cannot live without love!" And He was always waiting there to pour out more of His love to me. He will do the same for you if you are one of His children because He loves you, too.

After the disciples had chosen the ones who would minister to the widows, Peter said, **But we will give ourselves continually to prayer, and to the ministry of the word** (Acts 6:4). Most people do not know what it means to really minister the Word with signs and wonders in its fullness; but Peter said, *We will give ourselves*—that shows having control over and being the overseer of the new self. The disciples were overseers of themselves, and they gave themselves continually to prayer and to the ministry of the Word.

Jesus had left them the example of the Word and prayer. When He was here, He would talk to the Father; and the disciples could not keep up with Him in prayer. Instead of praying with Him in the Garden of Gethsemane, they fell asleep; and Jesus finally told them to sleep on. **Then cometh he** [Jesus] **to his disciples, and saith unto them, Sleep on now, and take your rest: behold, the hour is at hand, and the Son of man is betrayed into the hands of sinners** (Matthew 26:45).

It is hard to tell how many times Jesus called them out of sleep to pray when they walked with Him, and He was teaching them. How many times did He say, "Wake up; I have more to tell you!" or "Wake up; we must talk to our Father in Heaven"? Then He would leave them to spend the whole night talking to the Father while they slept.

GREAT, DIVINE POWER

When Jesus told the disciples to go to the Upper Room, He promised them that they would receive power. **Ye shall receive power, after that the Holy Ghost is come upon you** (Acts 1:8). Then after the disciples were full of the Holy Ghost, the Bible says they had great power. **And with great power gave the apostles witness of the resurrection of the Lord Jesus: and great grace was upon them all** (Acts 4:33).

We are to be witnesses to both the saved and the unsaved of the resurrection of Christ and of the salvation He brought. We are to be witnesses of freedom from all sin, the promises of God and the soon coming of the Lord. This verse also says that great grace was upon them all, so they had great power and great grace.

Jesus had the Holy Ghost with power, and you must have that great power working in you and through you, too. **God anointed Jesus of Nazareth with the Holy Ghost and with power** (Acts 10:38). When you are full of the Holy Ghost, you have not only power but great power.

Jesus had the greatness of everything. He knew what the Father wanted human beings to have, and He received it all and demonstrated how to use it as a human being with divinity inside. With divinity in our hearts, we too can do the things that Jesus did. He said, **Follow thou me** (John 21:22); and you must always keep that in mind.

Acts 10:38 goes on to say that Jesus **went about doing good, and healing all that were oppressed of the devil; for God was with**

him. When you are doing good, you are a testimony. You do not gossip because doing good does not include weak talk or serpent-talk; it includes only strong talk. When you are doing good, you have nothing to do with the devil.

Jesus healed all who were oppressed of the devil; but when you meet people who are oppressed, do you oppress and depress them even more by telling them a bit of gossip? We are to lift others up; so every time you push somebody down, you are in trouble. That will hinder you from getting your prayers through to Heaven and in anything else you do. It will also hinder God because He cannot give you His best or make plain paths for your feet when you will not walk them. If you want to go your own way, God is a wise God; and He will not lay out paths daily for you. If you did not walk His paths yesterday or last week, why should He lay out any more for you today?

Acts 10:38 ends with *for God was with Him.* When the angel told of Jesus' birth, he said that the child's name would be "Emanuel"; and that means God with us. **Behold, a virgin shall be with child, and shall bring forth a**

son, and they shall call his name Emmanuel, which being interpreted is, God with us (Matthew 1:23). You should never let a day go by without thinking, "God is with me."

STEPHEN WAS FULL OF THE SPIRIT

The Bible tells us that **Stephen, full of faith and power, did great wonders and miracles among the people** (Acts 6:8). When you are full of the Holy Ghost, you are full of faith, power, wisdom and knowledge; and the people could not resist the knowledge and wisdom that Stephen had. **And they were not able to resist the wisdom and the spirit by which he spake** (Acts 6:10).

Because Stephen was full of the Holy Ghost, the Spirit gave him exactly what to say; and he preached the truth without compromise. **Ye stiffnecked and uncircumcised in heart and ears, ye do always resist the Holy Ghost: as your fathers did, so do ye. Which of the prophets have not your fathers persecuted? and they have slain them which shewed before of the coming of the Just One; of whom ye have been now the betrayers and murderers: Who have received the**

law by the disposition of angels, and have not kept it (Acts 7:51–53). Stephen told the people how ugly they were and how they had mistreated the Spirit of truth; and they proved he was right when they got mad and started throwing dust into the air, screaming blasphemous things and picking up stones to use to kill him. But Stephen had not compromised; he had given the truth to them just as the Lord had delivered it.

If Stephen had not been full of the Holy Ghost, the Spirit could not have used him to perform miracles or to be the first martyr. Stephen was not chosen because he was wealthy or well known—he was not even one of the apostles. God had chosen him because he had not only received the Holy Ghost, but he was full of the Holy Ghost daily.

As the people were gnashing on Stephen with their teeth, **he, being full of the Holy Ghost, looked up stedfastly into heaven** (Acts 7:55). This tells me that Stephen looked to Heaven more than he looked at the things of the Earth, and he was yielded more to God's will than to his own will. He was not looking to father, mother, brothers, sisters or even to the children of God to help him in that hour; he was looking to the Lord.

Stephen was not full of self, doubt, fear and disobedience or of doing the things that most people want to do in life because he had denied himself of everything. We do not know anything about his family—he may have had to give them all up, or he may have been disowned by them.

When you are full of the Holy Ghost, you have that steadfast look; and you will not let anything or anybody hinder you or keep you away from being full of the Holy Ghost. As Stephen looked steadfastly up to Heaven, did he see people who did not like him? No, and there were plenty of them gathered around. The stones were flying, but Stephen saw the glory of God; and that was not all—he saw **Jesus standing on the right hand of God** (Acts 7:55). Why could he see all of this?—because he had no room for anything but the Lord.

FOLLOW STEPHEN'S EXAMPLE

When you are full of the Holy Ghost, you have no room for self or anything else.

Everybody is put down where he or she needs to be in your life, and the Lord has top priority. You have Heaven's eyes and Heaven's sight, and you behold the glory of the Lord.

Stephen looked to Heaven and said, **Behold, I see the heavens opened, and the Son of man standing on the right hand of God** (Acts 7:56). I also have beheld the Lord's glory, and it is an amazing experience for Him to let you see as Stephen saw; but it made the people angry. **They cried out with a loud voice, and stopped their ears, and ran upon him with one accord** (Acts 7:57). If the devil can get people into such one accord, why can't God through His Holy Spirit get us into one accord? It is because the old self and the devil match so well together.

And [they] **cast him out of the city, and stoned him: and the witnesses laid down their clothes at a young man's feet, whose name was Saul** [later to be the great Apostle Paul]. **And they stoned Stephen, calling upon God, and saying, Lord Jesus, receive my spirit. And he kneeled down, and cried with a loud voice, Lord, lay not this sin to**

their charge. And when he had said this, he fell asleep (Acts 7:58–60). The Lord had won! The devil tried to make the people think they had won, but Stephen died in exactly the same spirit that Jesus had died in—praying for those who were killing him and asking the Father to forgive them. That was divine forgiveness, not human forgiveness. It is not within the human spirit to forgive people who are stoning you to death, and you would not even be thinking about praying for them if you were in great pain.

What a witness Stephen made. He was full of the Holy Ghost, and all the Lord used him for flows like mighty rivers to children of God today—his obedience, his love and his spirit of no compromise. Stephen was so young, but that did not matter. The thing that stands out and says it all is that he was full of the Holy Ghost.

Stephen's death scattered the Christians in all directions; and the devil thought he was winning, but he was not. Stephen's death just sent the disciples beyond with the Gospel. **And at that time there was a great persecution**

against the church which was at Jerusalem; and they were all scattered abroad throughout the regions of Judaea and Samaria, except the apostles. Therefore they that were scattered abroad went everywhere preaching the word (Acts 8:1,4).

The Christians did not talk about how terrible it was that Stephen had died or that the authorities were after them to take their lives. The disciples were joyfully delivering the message that Stephen had died for. They knew it was real; and if they had ever had one doubt, it was all gone because Stephen had said, "I see Jesus."

THE EARLY CHURCH REVIVAL

Philip was not just filled with the Holy Ghost; he was full and running over, and the Lord wanted it to run over in Samaria. **Then Philip went down to the city of Samaria, and preached Christ unto them. And the people with one accord gave heed unto those things which Philip spake, hearing and seeing the miracles which he did. For unclean spirits, crying with loud voice, came out of many that were possessed with**

them: and many taken with palsies, and that were lame, were healed. And there was great joy in that city (Acts 8:5–8).

There was a great pouring out of the Spirit of God in Samaria. Devils were cast out; people were healed of all manner of sicknesses and diseases, and outstanding miracles took place because Philip was full of the Holy Ghost.

When the apostles at Jerusalem heard about what was happening in Samaria, they sent Peter and John there so the people could receive the Holy Ghost. **Now when the apostles which were at Jerusalem heard that Samaria had received the word of God, they sent unto them Peter and John: Who, when they were come down, prayed for them, that they might receive the Holy Ghost: (For as yet he was fallen upon none of them: only they were baptized in the name of the Lord Jesus.) Then laid they their hands on them, and they received the Holy Ghost** (Acts 8:14–17).

We do not know why Peter and John were chosen to go to Samaria, possibly just to be witnesses. Regardless, they went there and proved that people could receive the Holy Ghost by the laying on of hands.

In Samaria, there was a man, Simon the sorcerer, who was bewitching the people. **And when Simon saw that through laying on of the apostles' hands the Holy Ghost was given, he offered them money, Saying, Give me also this power, that on whomsoever I lay hands, he may receive the Holy Ghost. But Peter said unto him, Thy money perish with thee, because thou hast thought that the gift of God may be purchased with money. Thou hast neither part nor lot in this matter: for thy heart is not right in the sight of God. Repent therefore of this thy wickedness, and pray God, if perhaps the thought of thine heart may be forgiven thee** (Acts 8:18–22). We still have witches today who are bewitching people, and it is terrible.

Simon wanted the power the disciples had; and today, there are people who want the power I have. They will come to my services to search it out, but I pour the divine blood on their heads; and if they are not really there on business for God, they flee. Others will stay and get delivered, and we have had as many as fifteen witchdoctors delivered in one crusade.

All of this is real, so we have to have the leadership and the power of the Holy Ghost. Philip had that power; and when the people received the gift of the Holy Ghost, the revival was on. The Gospel continued to spread because God had people who went forward with the truth no matter what. They had enough of God to keep them moving, and they treasured the power of God in their lives more than they treasured life itself. They counted it as no life without the Spirit, and it is something indeed to have the greatness of God moving in such an unbelievable way.

THE HOLY GHOST SEPARATES

Barnabas was full of the Holy Ghost. **For he** [Barnabas] **was a good man, and full of the Holy Ghost and of faith: and much people was added unto the Lord** (Acts 11:24). One of the fruits of the Spirit is goodness, and Barnabas was a good man; so it is no wonder that the Lord used him. He was full of love because he could not be full of faith without being full of love; you cannot separate divine faith and divine love.

Many people were added unto the Lord because Barnabas was full of the Holy Ghost; and that made him full of faith, love and compassion for the lost. **And the hand of the Lord was with them: and a great number believed, and turned unto the Lord** (Acts 11:21). The hand of the Lord was upon them as they preached to the Grecians, and a great number of those people believed and turned to the Lord. When you are full of the Holy Ghost, the hand of the Lord is with you all the time.

Later, the Holy Ghost said, **Separate me Barnabas and Saul for the work whereunto I have called them** (Acts 13:2). Notice this, and many people do not pick it up—the Holy Ghost said, "Separate me." That means "separate for me." In other words, the Spirit was saying, "Separate Barnabas and Saul (who was later called Paul) from everything for me," and they did that. The disciples fasted and prayed, and they had the mind and the power of the Spirit to separate Barnabas and Paul unto the Lord and to anoint them.

Barnabas and Paul were willing to be given;

and the disciples gave them completely into the Lord's hands with all of God's love, faith and goodness. They separated them unto the Holy Ghost, separated them from any responsibilities or obligations they might have had to the people or to themselves. When they did that, it was wonderful; and they ordained them for the mission.

Again, I say that the Holy Ghost told the disciples to do this. The Spirit talks, but people don't always listen. Many times, man gets to the place where he feels, "I can do whatever I please. I can take care of this person, and I have a good plan for that situation"; but it just does not work like that. We must listen to the Spirit; and the Bible says seven times, **He that hath an ear, let him hear what the Spirit saith** (Revelation 2:7,11,17,29; 3:6,13,22). You have to have your ears tuned into Heaven or you will not go on the one flight out.

PAUL FOUGHT A GOOD FIGHT

A certain man named Demetrius, a silversmith, which made silver shrines for Diana, brought no small gain unto the craftsmen; Whom he called together with

the workmen of like occupation, and said, Sirs, ye know that by this craft we have our wealth. Moreover ye see and hear, that not alone at Ephesus, but almost throughout all Asia, this Paul hath persuaded and turned away much people, saying that they be no gods, which are made with hands: So that not only this our craft is in danger to be set at nought (Acts 19:24–27). The craftsman decided that something had to be done about Paul, and that was one reason why Paul was so persecuted.

Has the devil been after you? If not, it is not because you are immune to him; it is because you are not close enough to God to make the devil want to try to tantalize you. The closer to God you are, the more devils you will have to fight. Now, don't let that make you afraid to move on in because if you stay outside, the devil will get you anyway; so you had better move.

Paul had moved on in; and he wrote to Timothy, **For I am now ready to be offered, and the time of my departure is at hand. I have fought a good fight, I have finished**

my course, I have kept the faith (II Timothy 4:6,7). Paul knew he was at war, and he warned Timothy to be a good soldier. **Thou therefore endure hardness, as a good soldier of Jesus Christ. No man that warreth entangleth himself with the affairs of this life; that he may please him who hath chosen him to be a soldier** (II Timothy 2:3,4). Paul was telling Timothy to stay full of the Holy Ghost; and when he separated, he was to stay separated.

Paul had evidently known Timothy from the time he was just a child, and he loved him so much that he called him his very own son in the Lord. **To Timothy, my dearly beloved son: Grace, mercy, and peace, from God the Father and Christ Jesus our Lord** (II Timothy 1:2). Paul knew Timothy had been taught the Word as a child. **I call to remembrance the unfeigned faith that is in thee, which dwelt first in thy grandmother Lois, and thy mother Eunice; and I am persuaded that in thee also** (II Timothy 1:5).

Only through divine faith could Paul have gone through all he did, and you will not be able to go victoriously through all you will have to face without that same divine faith. The Bible says, **God hath dealt to every man the measure of faith** (Romans 12:3); and any time you need another measure of faith, you can have it. There is no limit on divine faith.

USE WHAT YOU HAVE FROM GOD

Jesus was the first person we have record of who was given the Spirit without measure. **For he** [Jesus] **whom God hath sent speaketh the words of God: for God giveth not the Spirit by measure unto him** (John 3:34). The Spirit is not being measured to the Church of Jesus Christ today, either; you can have as much of Him as you want—all that you will accept, all that you will believe for, all that you will obey for, all that you will be consecrated and dedicated for. It all depends on how much of yourself you give daily to the Lord.

The Lord wills all things to you; but if you do not give all of yourself to Him, you will not enjoy all of His inheritance. You will only use part of the inheritance, and that is sad when you need it all. Jesus knew He needed it all, and He was always victorious; no power could defeat Him. He held on to God no matter what people did to Him. You may say that the reason Jesus was not defeated was because He had come down from Heaven; but Paul was not defeated, and he did not come down from Heaven.

Before Paul was saved, he had come more from hell than he had from Heaven because he told Timothy he had been the chief of sinners. **This is a faithful saying, and worthy of all acceptation, that Christ Jesus came into the world to save sinners; of whom I am chief** (I Timothy 1:15). Paul was a mean man who had committed murder and blasphemed against the Lord, but he said he had received forgiveness because he had done those things in ignorance. **And I thank Christ Jesus our Lord, who hath enabled me, for that he counted me faithful, putting me into the ministry; Who was before a blasphemer, and a persecutor, and injurious: but I obtained mercy, because I did it ignorantly in unbelief** (I Timothy 1:12,13).

People will not have that excuse today because the Lord is shining the light on their paths. **And the times of this ignorance God winked at; but now commandeth all men everywhere to repent** (Acts 17:30). There was a time when God winked at ignorance, but now He is calling everybody to repentance. Jesus said, **Except ye repent, ye shall all likewise perish** (Luke 13:3).

Paul was full of the Holy Ghost while he lived and while he was facing death. Some people become very religious at the end of their lives, but Paul had become religious long before that. He was so full of the Holy Ghost that the things of God were like a deep well within him that kept overflowing, and Paul poured them out through all the books he wrote. The wells of salvation really overflowed for Paul, and the Holy Ghost flowed it out through him.

THE WIND OF THE SPIRIT

The true Church should be living and abiding in Bible Pentecost today, but so many have compromised to get the favor of man because they do not want the criticism of the world and the battles of persecution. They are not sailing anywhere on the sea of greatness, and they are not going out into the stormy deep to bring in the lost.

A ship with sails has to wait for the wind to blow before it can move, and we are like that, too. Just as the Early Church depended on the wind of the Spirit to move them and take them beyond the wrong influence of people, so must we.

When the wind of the Spirit came rushing into the Upper Room, it blew upon Simon Peter; and he became the great apostle of Pentecost. Simon, who had at one time been so weak and denied even knowing Jesus and had blasphemed His name to prove it, stood up and preached a great message to the people in Acts 2:14–36. Peter had been forgiven, and his sins were under the blood; but he did not know he was going to be the one chosen to be the spokesman. So when you think the Spirit is not moving for you, do not try to move your ship on your own. Just wait for the wind of the Spirit to blow; and in due season, your ship will move.

The wind of the Spirit took the Early Church disciples beyond the world and even beyond their own families who had fought against them, disinherited them and put them to shame. Their family members testified against them and even had them put to death, but the saints waited on the Spirit. They hid in caves and covered themselves with animal skins to disguise themselves when they would go out to look for food.

The Bible says the world was not worthy of those saints. **Who through faith subdued kingdoms, wrought righteousness, obtained promises, stopped the mouths of lions. Quenched the violence of fire, escaped the edge of the sword, out of weakness were made strong, waxed valiant in fight, turned to flight the armies of the aliens. Women received their dead raised to life again: and others were tortured, not accepting deliverance; that they might obtain a better resurrection: And others had trial of cruel mockings and scourgings, yea, moreover of bonds and imprisonment: They were stoned, they were sawn asunder, were tempted, were slain with the sword: they wandered**

about in sheepskins and goatskins; being destitute, afflicted, tormented; (Of whom the world was not worthy:) they wandered in deserts, and in mountains, and in dens and caves of the earth. And these all, having obtained a good report through faith, received not the promise: God having provided some better thing for us, that they without us should not be made perfect (Hebrews 11:33–40). The Lord decreed that Heaven is for that kind of person.

When Jesus came, it was a takeover; and although it looked like Jesus had not left much of an impact, He had paid for all the power people would need to defeat the devil. For the first thirty-three years of the Church, the true disciples used that same power; and the devil could not stop them. The more he persecuted them, the more the truth went forth. When the devil comes against you, let him cause you to do more for God than ever before.

WAIT ON THE SPIRIT

Through Samuel, the Lord told David to wait for the wind of the Spirit to move in the tops of the mulberry trees before he went to battle. If he had moved before he had heard the tops of the trees rustle, he would have moved without God because the Lord had said, **And let it be, when thou hearest the sound of a going in the tops of the mulberry trees, that then thou shalt bestir thyself: for then shall the LORD go out before thee, to smite the host of the Philistines** (II Samuel 5:24).

The enemy was waiting for David; so if he had gone before the Spirit or the wind stirred, his army would have been destroyed. The wind of the Spirit is power.

Many people have not waited for the wind of the Spirit, and they have gone into fanaticism and done things that have brought reproach on the Lord. Paul said that people were puffed up with ego in his day, and they are still like that today. **But I will come to you shortly, if the Lord will, and will know, not the speech of them which are puffed up, but the power. For the kingdom of God is not in word, but in power** (I Corinthians 4:19,20). Paul was saying, "I will not know the speech of them who are full of ego but of those who have the power of the Holy Ghost—they are the ones

I will listen to. I don't care what you puffed-up ones have to say, and I would not believe it anyway because you are liable to say anything." Those who are full of ego should record what they say when they are puffed up. Paul said that *the Kingdom of God is not in word but in power,* so puffed-up people cannot use it. In fact, you can puff up until you puff yourself right out of God's presence and out of His Kingdom.

What is the remedy for ego? You have to take a big dose of the Holy Ghost every time you start to puff up with ego, and it will cure you instantly. If you already have the divine blood in your soul, take a big dose of the Holy Ghost and let Him have His way. He will pump the blood into your mind and take out all of the ego.

God did not allow Moses to enter the land of Canaan because he had failed to sanctify the Lord one time. Moses was angry with the Israelites when they complained about not having water; and he said, **Must we fetch you water out of this rock** (Numbers 20:10)? Instead, he should have sanctified God and said, "Must

God bring water out of this rock for you people?" As it turned out, Moses only missed out on a lot of sorrow and heartache because the people continued to be disobedient and rebellious even after they had entered the land of Canaan. But I know his heart must have been set on going with them into Canaan.

The Lord still loved Moses, but God had to abide by the Law that He had set forth. Moses had been the lawgiver, so the Lord certainly could not compromise with him. Moses did not mean to take the Lord's glory; he was so humble, and he did not have that kind of spirit. He said what he did because the Israelites had pressed him into it.

USE DIVINE POWER

In this final hour, your spiritual power will be tested. When you are facing great trials and you wonder what is happening to you, you must know that your spiritual power is being tested; and you should be glad that it is. How would you know whether or not your faith is any good if it is never tried? "Talking faith" will not work.

God's people will be tried and persecuted;

so when you are going through a valley, just cry, "Hallelujah! My spiritual power is being tested, and I have all the confidence of Heaven in it. I know it is fine because I know I am full of the Spirit and full of His power, love, grace and faith." You can never have too much Holy Ghost power, so never be afraid to get refilled whenever you need more.

God's work can be done only by the Spirit's power working through a consecrated heart and life. The reason why there has not been more work done for the Lord in our day is because so many people do not yield to the Spirit. They neglect Him, fight Him, and many of them will not even receive Him.

Samson had the power of God, but he did not keep it. **And she** [Delilah] **said unto him** [Samson], **How canst thou say, I love thee, when thine heart is not with me? thou hast mocked me these three times, and hast not told me wherein thy great strength lieth. And it came to pass, when she pressed him daily with her words, and urged him, so that his soul was vexed unto death; That he told her all his heart, and said unto her,**

There hath not come a razor upon mine head; for I have been a Nazarite unto God from my mother's womb: if I be shaven, then my strength will go from me, and I shall become weak, and be like any other man. And when Delilah saw that he had told her all his heart, she sent and called for the lords of the Philistines, saying, Come up this once, for he hath shewed me all his heart. Then the lords of the Philistines came up unto her, and brought money in their hand. And she made him sleep upon her knees; and she called for a man, and she caused him to shave off the seven locks of his head; and she began to afflict him, and his strength went from him. And she said, The Philistines be upon thee, Samson. And he awoke out of his sleep, and said, I will go out as at other times before, and shake myself. And he wist not that the LORD was departed from him. But the Philistines took him, and put out his eyes, and brought him down to Gaza, and bound him with fetters of brass; and he did grind in the prison house (Judges 16:15–21).

Samson was accustomed to shaking himself to stir up the power of God, but the shake was not the power; the power came from the power of the Holy Ghost. When Samson sinned against God, the Holy Spirit departed from him; and he did not know it. So instead of the Holy Spirit taking Samson over, the enemy took him over; and that was so sad.

When a person becomes strong in his own strength, the Holy Spirit departs. That is a profound statement. When you become strong in the might of your own power, you have left God out; and when you leave God out of your life, the Holy Ghost departs because you are using self.

REALITY IN THE SPIRIT

What good has Calvary done for you unless you have come into a personal relationship with Christ to the point that you are willing to suffer? You will never be willing to sacrifice for the Lord until you come into the reality of the price Jesus paid and all He went through for you.

What power has Pentecost brought you unless you have come into a personal relationship with the Holy Ghost? What worth is He to you if He is not real to you? When I received the Holy Ghost, He became my whole world. He elevated me into lofty heights day after day as I spent much time with Him. The Lord would speak to my heart, and it was marvelous to hear the Holy Spirit singing in many different tongues and dialects through me. I was so thrilled with Him, and He was just as real to me as my own hands and body were.

The power of the Spirit has to be just as real to you as the forgiveness of sins is through the blood of the Lamb, but you have to let Him be that real. For so many people, their salvation is real; but they sometimes forget about the personality of the Holy Spirit and the reality of Him. You cannot just have the reality of salvation; you must also have the reality of the person of the Holy Spirit living and dwelling on the inside of you.

This Jesus ministry has the real power of God with signs, wonders, miracles and healings. The Lord organized and ordained this work, and it is to be a continuation of the

Early Church—we have taken up where the book of Acts left off. We are carrying the Gospel to the world through the power of the Holy Ghost, and we are going right on through to Rapture ground.

YOU MUST SEPARATE

The Bible tells you to commit your ways unto the Lord. **Commit thy way unto the LORD; trust also in him; and he shall bring it to pass** (Psalm 37:5). You have to take the Lord's ways, but you cannot have the way of the Lord only when you want it and then have your own way at other times; that will not work. It is one thing to form your own plans, and then ask for the Lord's guidance; but it is quite another thing to trust Him to form your plans.

Don't always look at other people, and spend no time around those who are not consecrated and dedicated. Young People, you must separate from the spirit of the world if you have not already done so. You need to get it all out of your system and then shun those worldly spirits and go after God. You must talk about the Lord.

Even when I was in theological school, I had to separate from those students who carried on with a bunch of foolishness—teasing, joking and speaking idle talk. Those of us who were dedicated and consecrated were the ones who would help people to get saved, and then we would pray them through to the Holy Ghost. We could be called out of bed at any time, and we were willing to stay up all night if need be just to help someone who needed to receive the Holy Ghost. Those of us who separated made a difference and became great influences, and we were able to convince others to become dedicated and to have a desire for the real thing.

THE SPIRIT MAKES WINNERS

The Holy Spirit didn't start baptizing people in any great way until the Day of Pentecost; but even in Old Testament days, He was always there. God told me that the Holy Ghost was there with Him and His Son when they made the first man and woman in Eden. The Holy Spirit was with Abraham or he never would have gone to the mount to offer Isaac. **By faith Abraham, when he was tried,**

offered up Isaac; and he that had received the promises offered up his only begotten son, Of whom it was said, That in Isaac shall thy seed be called: Accounting that God was able to raise him up, even from the dead; from whence also he received him in a figure (Hebrews 11:17–19). *You will not give all like Abraham did, saith the Lord, unless you have the Holy Spirit upon you, in you and directing you. He releases the divine faith you have.*

If Gideon had not had the Holy Ghost with him, he never would have won; and the army of God would have been defeated. Twenty-two thousand of Gideon's soldiers turned back at one time because they were fearful at heart; and still, the Lord told him he had too many men to give him the victory. Why?—because the Lord wanted all the glory. **And the LORD said unto Gideon, The people that are with thee are too many for me to give the Midianites into their hands, lest Israel vaunt themselves against me, saying, Mine own hand hath saved me. Now therefore go to, proclaim in the ears of the**

people, saying, Whosoever is fearful and afraid, let him return and depart early from mount Gilead. And there returned of the people twenty and two thousand; and there remained ten thousand. And the LORD said unto Gideon, The people are yet too many (Judges 7:2–4).

Gideon won, but he won with only 300 men. **And the LORD said unto Gideon, By the three hundred men that lapped will I save you, and deliver the Midianites into thine hand** (Judges 7:7). It does not matter how many people there are but how much those people yield to the Holy Spirit and what God can do with them. The Holy Spirit is greater than the spirit of the devil and all his demons, and you must remember that.

Through the Holy Ghost, Elijah and Enoch won—they went to Heaven alive! Moses won with signs, wonders, miracles and healings through the pillar of fire, the fire of the Holy Ghost; *and that is the only way we are going to win, saith the Lord.* Remember that Pharaoh's army was completely destroyed. **And Moses stretched forth his hand over the sea, and**

the sea returned to his strength when the morning appeared; and the Egyptians fled against it; and the LORD overthrew the Egyptians in the midst of the sea. And the waters returned, and covered the chariots, and the horsemen, and all the host of Pharaoh that came into the sea after them; there remained not so much as one of them. But the children of Israel walked upon dry land in the midst of the sea; and the waters were a wall unto them on their right hand, and on their left (Exodus 14:27–29).

When Jesus was on Earth, He finished His work and won through the Holy Ghost. Shortly before He was crucified, He said to the Father, **I have finished the work which thou gavest me to do** (John 17:4). Then He cried on the Cross, **It is finished: and he bowed his head, and gave up the ghost** (John 19:30).

After Jesus had been resurrected, He ascended to Heaven and carried the divine blood down the Avenue of Glory. He stopped before the throne and poured out the blood that He had shed for our sins to be washed away and for our sicknesses to be cured saying, "Father, I won! I have done what you sent me to do." The Bride of Christ will also be able to say, "We won! We have finished the work, Father, which you ordained us to do. We didn't miss a soul you had marked for us to win." We can only finish our work through the Holy Ghost.

GIVE YOURSELF TO THE HOLY GHOST

I would never be where I am today if it had not been for the Holy Ghost baptism. It changed my life completely, and the Spirit is the preacher. When I preached my first sermon, I didn't know I was going to preach. My head went into a glory cloud that covered me to my waist, and I had never even seen a glory cloud before. Then the Holy Ghost took me over, and I was preaching without even realizing it. When I sat down, the Lord spoke to me and said, "That was your first sermon." When the pastor heard about it, he wanted me to preach that Saturday night. I did, and I tore down the walls of Jericho for him and for all the others who were there. We had a great time that night!

That was the first time I had ever preached in that pastor's services, and his people loved hearing my messages so much that he started letting me preach on Sunday mornings. That same pastor said, "If Jesus tarries and this young man grows up, he is going to be something special in the world." I have thought about that again and again, and that was a prophecy that God had given to him.

Thus saith the Lord, I am the Lord; I gave this message. My servant didn't think it up; I gave it to him, and he gave it to you. Now, you are responsible for it. My coming is upon you. Get ready, saith the Lord. Yield and give over your soul, mind and body and be bathed in the Spirit. Let my Spirit comfort you. Let my Spirit guide you, saith the Lord. Receive ye the Holy Ghost.

A MESSAGE FROM THE HOLY SPIRIT

Thus saith the Spirit, I have worked with you day and night. I have flowed God's love to you, but you have not used it. I have flowed faith to you, but you have not used it. I have dealt with you again and again, and I have given you wisdom and knowledge. I am the Spirit of truth, and I have given you His truth; but you have not accepted it.

I have been sent on a divine mission just for you, to prepare you for this hour. I have been sent to you to dwell and live on the inside of you. I have told you of your disobedience. I have told you of your envy and strife. I have told you of your contentions; and yet, you will not listen. You have grieved and grieved me, the Spirit of truth that dwells within. Patiently, I have worked with you; but you will not follow the truth, and you will not walk in the truth. That is the reason some of you are not free, and you are in bondage; and the Lord will not be able to leap with you.

But some of you are ready; you have been made ready. You have yielded to the truth. You have yielded to everlasting love and eternal faith. You have yielded to the ways of the Lord. You have made your crooked paths straight, and you are on the narrow road. You have passed through the strait gate, and you are on the road of love. That love flows in your soul, and I am able to shed it abroad in your minds daily. I am able to use the living water to flush from

your minds that which hinders and worries you. I am able to pour strength into your mind, and I am able to flow wisdom and knowledge to you.

I have come to serve. I have come to be your helper. I have come to teach you; but if you will not listen, you cannot learn. Some of you have listened, and I rejoice and rejoice and rejoice with you because you have listened. Some of you are pure and clean and spotless, and Heaven is delighted. The hour has now come, your hour of victory; but if you do not make it your hour of victory, it will be your hour of greatest defeat.

My Spirit cannot always strive with you. Take heed to your ways. Look into the truth and see yourself—that is the only place you will see yourself as you really are. Use the Word; it is your only safety. Use the Word; it is your power of deliverance. See yourself as God sees you, and then make that which is wrong to be right through the blood of the only begotten Son of God.

I call to you. Open your ears and hear

what I am saying to you. I came to prepare a bride for Jesus, and my mission will soon be finished, saith the Spirit of the Lord. I have done all that I can do; now it is left up to you. You must have the veil given to you through His shed blood, the veil of separation; and only the blood can separate you from all sin. Only the blood can separate you from the world. Only the blood can separate you from everything that is unlike your Lord and separate you unto Himself... only the blood.

Hear what the Spirit is saying, and I am saying much in this your final hour. I am warning you daily. All of God's power is being used for you because destruction is just ahead, disaster is just ahead. Some of you are so close to eternity, but you do not know it because you will not listen to the truth; and that is the reason you are in bondage. God has sent the truth to you, crieth the Spirit; and the Spirit of truth is to dwell on the inside of you at all times. If you do not accept the truth, you will not accept the Spirit of truth; and the Lord will allow you to believe a lie and be damned because you will not accept the truth about yourself.

I call to you; yield to my Spirit. I call to you who are walking in the love of your Lord, you who have been made free of all the spots and the wrinkles. You are free all because of the blood, and I say to you that all the courage of Heaven is yours; all the love of Heaven is yours; all the faith of Heaven is yours, and all the power of Heaven is yours. There is nothing for you to ever fear because He who conquered all the powers of the devil walks with you. He is your Beloved; and you are His beloved, saith the Spirit of the Lord unto this people.

About the Author

Reverend Ernest Angley is the pastor and founder of Ernest Angley Ministries with churches in two locations: Ernest Angley's Grace Cathedral in Cuyahoga Falls, Ohio and Grace Cathedral in Akron, Ohio (Springfield Township). This Jesus ministry is in the midst of a tremendous worldwide outreach which is spreading the Gospel into many nations by way of crusades, television and the printed page. God has endowed Reverend Angley with special gifts to bring healing for soul, mind and body to people all over the world. He does not claim to be a healer but a witness to the marvelous healing power of Christ. His television programs—"The Ernest Angley Hour" (aired weekly) and "The Ninety and Nine Club" (aired daily)—present the fullness of God's Word and teach the truth about salvation, healing and the baptism in the Holy Ghost.

Check your local listing for times in your area.

Visit our website at ErnestAngley.org

by Ernest Angley

RAPTURED

A novel by Ernest Angley about the second coming of Christ based on biblical facts. This timely book could change your life. Price: **$3.50**

FAITH IN GOD HEALS THE SICK

An instructive book by Ernest Angley telling not only how to receive physical healing from the Lord, but also how to keep that healing. Price: **$1.95**

UNTYING GOD'S HANDS

With amazing frankness the author has dealt with many controversial subjects in this book: the ministry of angels, preparation required for the Rapture, guidelines for dating, sex in marriage, sex outside marriage, masturbation, homosexuality. Many other subjects covering the whole life of man are woven into the underlying theme of how to untie God's hands. Price: **$10.00**

CELL 15

The dramatic true story of the imprisonment of Reverend Ernest Angley in Munich, Germany, for preaching the Gospel and praying for the sick. Price: **$2.95**

GOD'S RAINBOW OF PROMISES

Precious promises from the Word of God (KJV) to cover your every need now and forever will enhance your personal devotions and prove a great blessing in time of trouble. Price: **$1.95**

THE DECEIT OF LUCIFER

Using the Word of God as the only standard, Reverend Angley strips the camouflage of Lucifer's insidious deceit from demonology, seducing spirits and the counterfeit works of God. A culmination of information derived from years of training by the Holy Spirit, this book is a must for anyone who wishes to recognize the deadly pitfalls of the dangerous end-time hour in which we live. Price: **$10.00**

LEECHING OF THE MIND

Like parasitic leeches of the jungle that live off the blood of their victims, leeches of the mind sap the life force of reason. Through the gifts of the Holy Spirit, Reverend Angley exposes the inner working of Lucifer in the human mind, revealing the most incredible takeover by Lucifer a person could suffer other than total devil possession of the soul. Price: **$10.00**

THE POWER OF BIBLE FASTING

The Power Of Bible Fasting is one of the most thorough books on Bible fasting ever written, an invaluable guide into a deeper walk with God and the reality of His presence. Price: **$10.00**

LOVE IS THE ROAD

Through His great and precious promises we receive much from the Lord on His Love Road. The Love Road is a supernatural Road laid out by supernatural power, planned by the Lord God Almighty. Discover how you, too, can walk this marvelous Road into the fullness and greatness of God in this last and final hour. Price: **$10.00**

WEEDS IN EDEN

One of God's greatest disappointments was finding weeds in Eden. *Weeds in Eden* describes the cost to God and man of minds overrun with the weeds of disobedience and rebellion. The price paid by Heaven and Earth was sorrow, heartache and despair, and the price today is still the same. Let this book help you search out any weeds that would contaminate the Eden of your mind in this last and final hour. Price: **$10.00**

THE UNFORGIVABLE SIN

There is a sin not even Calvary can pardon. Once people commit this sin, only doom and damnation await them with no chance ever of Heaven. Jesus said, *All manner of sin and blasphemy shall be forgiven unto men, but the blasphemy against the Holy Ghost shall not be forgiven unto men . . . neither in this world, neither in the world to come* (Matthew 12:31, 32) Price: **$10.00**

PROSPERITY: SPIRITUAL, PHYSICAL, FINANCIAL...

To bring forth the fullness of God's prosperity that we find in His divine will, the writer has gone into the deepness of the Holy Spirit and the Word of God. Prosperity for soul, mind and body is God's will for all His Children. Price: **$10.00**

REALITY OF THE BLOOD: VOL. 1

In this enlightened book on divine blood, the unique and insightful author, through the power of the Holy Ghost, opens up amazing revelations about the importance of the blood of Jesus for all people. Those who love God with all their heart will be thrilled to find the marvelous understanding of the blood that has been set down in this book. Price: **$10.00**

REALITY OF THE BLOOD: VOL. 2

They used the Blood . . . We must use the Blood

The power in the divine blood of Jesus is being presented in living reality as multitudes experience miracles of healing for soul, mind and body. The Early Church used divine blood through the power of the Holy Ghost; now it's time for the Church in this last and final hour to use the power in the divine blood. Price: **$10.00**

REALITY OF THE BLOOD: VOL. 3

Faith and Feelings!

Through the Spirit of God recognize the difference between feelings and faith. Feelings can dishearten you if you rely on them to determine your benefits with God and what you should do for Him. Trusting in feelings is the reason so many Christians have battles of the mind. Price: **$10.00**

REALITY OF THE BLOOD: VOL. 4

Blood Victory Over Disappointments!

Realize what is yours through divine blood: freedom from depression, oppression, sin, sickness, disease and all other bondages of the devil. Through divine blood it is possible to overcome Satan's great weapon of disappointments and take on the mind of Jesus. Price: **$10.00**

REALITY OF THE BLOOD: VOL. 5

Don't Waste The Blood!

Jesus shed His precious blood on Calvary for a lost and dying world, and He intends for us to use it. That blood is man's most powerful weapon, and we must not waste even one, tiny drop. In this profound end-time teaching, Reverend Angley shares an incredible revelation from the Lord on how to use the divine blood to spray the devil into defeat every day. This book will completely change your life! Price: **$10.00**

THE REALITY OF THE PERSON OF THE HOLY SPIRIT: VOL. 1

The Holy Spirit in Types and Shadows

Reverend Angley lifts the mist curtains of the Old Testament to reveal the Holy Spirit in types and shadows. Let these marvelous types and shadows come alive in your heart and thrill your very being. Price: **$10.00**

THE REALITY OF THE PERSON OF THE HOLY SPIRIT: VOL. 2

The Holy Spirit and Fire

The fire of the Holy Spirit includes great miracles of deliverance as well as the devouring fire of judgment. Read how the fire of the Holy Spirit will affect your life. Price: **$10.00**

THE REALITY OF THE PERSON OF THE HOLY SPIRIT: VOL. 3

The Holy Spirit in the New and Old Testaments

The Holy Spirit worked throughout the New Testament, but did He work in Old Testament days? Yes, He did. Read about it in volume 3 of the Holy Spirit series. Price: **$10.00**

THE REALITY OF THE PERSON OF THE HOLY SPIRIT: VOL. 4

The Mantle of Power

The Bible is filled with examples of the Holy Ghost using the mantle of power through godly men and women. All the truth of God as well as His power is in the mantle. Recognize the blood strength, the greatness, wisdom and knowledge in the glorious mantle of power - and it's for all who will accept it! Price: **$10.00**

HURRY FRIDAY!

Autobiography of Ernest Angley

Hurry Friday! will make you laugh, cry, and rejoice in the amazing way God has moved in the life of this unique servant of God. Hard cover price: **$30.00** Paperback price: **$20.00**

THE MIND OF CHRIST

Let this mind be in you, which was also in Christ (Philippians 2:5). What made up His mind? Listed in this book are 141 ingredients found in the mind of Christ. Price: **$10.00**

LIVING FREE FROM SIN: VOL. 1

Is eternal security conditional or unconditional? Can people really live free from sin? This ground-breaking study delves deep into the Scriptures to shed light on a damnable doctrine spreading throughout the world today and reveals what the Bible really has to say about this subject. Price: **$10.00**

LIVING FREE FROM SIN: VOL. 2

The Bible is filled with the message of Living Free From Sin, and this second volume continues the study of this much-neglected subject. Scripture by scripture, the Lord continues to uncover the damnable doctrine of eternal security in Paul's writings to the Romans, the Corinthians and the Philippians. Price: **$10.00**

BATTLES OF THE MIND

Are you tormented with Battles of the Mind? Do you fight depression, oppression, despair and mental misgivings? Are you tormented with the past, present and future or bound with stifling doubt and fear? This book gives you the Bible cure for all that Battles Your Mind! Price: **$10.00**

HEALING FROM HEAVEN, VOL. 1

God's Word promises healing for soul, mind and body to all people; and that healing comes straight from Heaven. If you're in need of a miracle, this one-of-a-kind miracle manual will show you that you can be made whole. It takes you step-by-step through the different healing methods and then teaches you how to receive and keep your miracle. Price: **$10.00**

HEALING FROM HEAVEN, VOL. 2

The Wheel in the Middle of the Wheel

Few writers have understood or ever dealt with Ezekiel's vision of the wheels, and this book reveals the true meaning of that great vision. You will come to know Jesus, the Wheel in the middle of the wheels, like you have never known Him before; and you will learn how to make sure that every aspect of your life is turning in unison with Him. Price: **$10.00**

ARMAGEDDON

The novel Armageddon reveals the overwhelming fear, torment, death and unimaginable destruction that will take place on Earth after the Rapture. The gripping story is based on 100% Bible truth, and the end times have never before been written about in such shocking reality. You must know about the coming Tribulation and the war to end all wars and heed God's warnings, or you will regret it for all eternity. Price: **$10.00**

Please allow 3-6 weeks for delivery.
If you haven't received books in this amount of time, write and let us know, and we will make sure they are sent right away.

IF YOUR BOOKSTORE DOES NOT STOCK THESE BOOKS, ORDER FROM ERNEST ANGLEY MINISTRIES, BOX 1790, AKRON, OHIO 44309

You may also order online at ErnestAngley.org

Name ______________________________

Address ______________________________

City ______________________________

State ______________________ Zip ______________

PLEASE SEND ME THE BOOKS INDICATED:

Qty. ___ B1 - Raptured - $3.50 ea

Qty. ___ B2 - Faith in God Heals the Sick - $1.95 ea

Qty. ___ B4 - Untying God's Hands - $10.00 ea

Qty. ___ B5 - Cell 15 - $2.95 ea

Qty. ___ B6 - God's Rainbow of Promises - $1.95 ea

Qty. ___ B7 - The Deceit of Lucifer - $10.00 ea

Qty. ___ B8 - Leeching of the Mind - $10.00 ea

Qty. ___ B9 - The Power of Bible Fasting - $10.00 ea

Qty. ___ B10 - Love is the Road - $10.00 ea

Qty. ___ B11 - Weeds In Eden - $10.00 ea

Qty. ___ B12 - The Unforgivable Sin - $10.00 ea

Qty. ___ B14 - Prosperity: Spiritual, Physical, Financial... - $10.00 ea

Qty. ___ B13 - Reality of the Blood, Vol. 1 - $10.00 ea

Qty. ___ B15 - Reality of the Blood, Vol. 2 - $10.00 ea

Continued